STANDING UP, SPEAKING OUT

40 Years of Fighting Injustice

MERVYN THOMAS

RIVER
PUBLISHING

River Publishing & Media Ltd

info@river-publishing.co.uk

www.river-publishing.co.uk

ISBN 978-1-908393-84-5

Printed in the United Kingdom by TJ International, Padstow, Cornwall

Contents

Dedication

This book is dedicated to my loving and long-suffering wife, Wendy, who has steadfastly stood by me for the last 26 years of this journey

What Others Are Saying...

"I first met Merv in 1985 on a trip to Romania and we quickly became firm friends. Since then, we have been united in our shared passion for freedom of religion and to be a voice for those who cannot speak for themselves. This book not only tells the story of a great friend with whom I have shared many adventures, it is testament to 40 years of campaigning for justice and freedom from oppression. I can't recommend it more highly."

Frank Wolf, Former US Congressman

"Mervyn Thomas is a living legend. For forty years he's been comforting the afflicted and afflicting the comfortable, reminding us of our responsibility to pray, to lobby and to fight for those who are persecuted for their faith. Countless lives have been changed by Mervyn's sheer bloody-minded resilience and faith. His story will inspire you with new hope, provoking you to engage in a mission that is sadly even more needed today than it was back in 1979 when the CSW adventure began."

Pete Greig, 24-7 Prayer International and Emmaus Rd, Guildford

"Having known and worked alongside Mervyn for the past ten years, I realise his heart and enthusiasm for justice and freedom, and his tireless efforts in ensuring that they are advocated for across the world, especially in those countries where the greatest violations can be found. Mervyn's vision and commitment have ensured that those needing the greatest support around the world are not forgotten and that their voices are clearly heard. It only takes the briefest of encounters with Mervyn to realise that what drives him to be a committed husband, father, colleague, advocate and friend is his unwavering Christian faith that underpins his entire being."

His Eminence Archbishop Angaelos, Coptic Orthodox Archbishop of London

"It is not a good time to be a religious minority in some countries. Pursuing a path to promote freedom and tolerance as an aid to a community's security and development, rather than a threat to it, is not easy, but it is essential. This engrossing read from the sharp end of such endeavour gives a flavour of the courage, commitment and extraordinary events which can occur on such a journey, to the huge credit of my friend Mervyn Thomas and CSW."

Rt Hon Alistair Burt MP, Minister of State for the Middle East at the Foreign & Commonwealth Office

"The word passion can be defined as 'the degree of difficulty we're willing to go to, to achieve our goal.' Looked at through that lens, I'd have to describe Mervyn Thomas as one of the most passionate people I've ever met. This book is an inspiring account of faith, persistence and resilience. It can be all too easy to ignore the battle, or shy away from it – but this is a story of those who have done just the opposite, and have run towards the battle with courage and conviction. Mervyn, Christian Solidarity Worldwide, and the heroes of faith featured in this book who they've advocated for, are an inspiration to us all. Beware, this could be a life-changing read!"

Matt Redman, songwriter and Grammy award winner

"*Standing Up, Speaking Out* is the personal story of a Christian pioneer who had a vision for Christian advocacy which was ahead of its time and now provides a leading light in Christian engagement in freedom of religion or belief."

Rev Joel Edwards, author, coach, Bible teacher and international inspirational speaker

Acknowledgements

In writing the story of both my life and that of CSW, inevitably I have left out the names of many people who have been very much part of my life's journey. I would therefore like to acknowledge some of them in this section of the book.

First, I pay tribute to my family, recognising the part they have played in loving and supporting me over the years. So, to Wendy, Vix, Seth, Meg and David, mother-in-law Pat, niece and nephew Alison and James and their families, brothers and sisters-in-law Sharon and George, Lisa and Matt and their families: thanks for always being there for me.

The Churchill Society has been a large part of my life for the past 41 years. We are a group of ageing young Conservatives who have stuck together since its formation in 1977. I have been their only Chairman, despite resigning at every AGM in living memory! Many of our members have sadly died, but those remaining (and not mentioned elsewhere) include Lady Valerie Bright, Tricia Gurnett, Pat and John Jannaway, Christopher Thompson, Suzarne Price, Mike Orriss, John Edwards, and Martin and Cathy Covill (Black Fen Faction).

For ten very happy years of my life I was part of a musical group called the Jesus Folk based in Thurrock. Annually we performed a Gospel-based musical at the Thameside Theatre in Grays. I always got to play the villain and loved every minute of it. We were led by the ubiquitous Dawn Bareham of the Salvation Army, and the cast members all became wonderful friends. I can't attempt to list them because inevitably I'll leave someone out! You know who you are and I love you all!

Over the years I have been privileged to work with many MPs and Peers. Those not mentioned elsewhere in the book, but deserving of thanks include Gary Streeter MP, Stephen Crabb MP, David Drew MP, Mr Speaker, John Bercow MP, Former MP's David Burrowes and Andy Reed, and former MEP Terry Wynn – all of whom have been very supportive in our promotion of Freedom of Religion or Belief (FORB).

Additionally, a very special mention must go to my friend Fiona Bruce MP, a small lady but an absolute giant in fighting for the right to religious freedom around the world, and many other righteous causes, for which she always speaks up so bravely and eloquently.

In the House of Lords special thanks must go to Lord Jimmy Gordon, Lord Andrew Green of Deddington, Lord Jonathan Evans, Lord Michael Bates and the Lord Bishop of Coventry, Christopher Cocksworth.

Over the years I have been supported by many people in prayer, but I must pay a very special tribute to my good friend and faithful prayer partner Simon Groves, and also to fellow members of the Brothers Prayer Group, Tom Benyon, Lord Michael Hastings, Jim Pringle, Alistair Burt MP, Michael Trend and Jonathan Aitken.

In the cause of collaboration, I am indebted to all my friends within the Religious Liberty Partnership and especially to my long term UK colleagues, Lisa Pearce of Open Doors and Paul Robinson of Release International – thanks for being so supportive in all you have done.

CSW Board of Trustees, David Taylor (Chairman), Anne Coles, Franklin Evans, Simon George, Michael Gibbons, Michael Gowen, Nigel Grinyer, Christian Guy, Dave Landrum, Ann-Marie Msichili, Yunusa Nmadu, Sarah Snyder and Claire Upton – are all staunchly committed to our work, and I would like to thank them for both their valuable personal support and their wise counsel.

Members of CSW board of reference

Shola Ameobi, Lord Donald Anderson, Rev Richard Bewes, Rev Lyndon Bowring, Viscount Brentford, Fiona Bruce MP, Alistair Burt MP, Gerald Coates, Roger Forster, John Glen MP, Simon Hughes, Canon J. John, Archbishop Benjamin Kwashi of Jos, Earl of Powis, Archbishop John Sentamu, Rev David Shoshanya, Julian Speroni, Charles Whitehead – all of whom have been fantastic cheer leaders for CSW and for the FORB cause generally.

I have benefitted so much from the wealth of religious freedom wisdom and expertise in the USA and I thank Dr Thomas Farr, Stephen McFarland,

Suzanne Scholte, Bob Fu, Lauren Homer, Michael Farris, Knox Thames, Brent McBurney, Tina Ramirez, Tiffany Noelle Barrans, Scott Flipse, Elyse Anderson, Abby Berg, Ambassadors John Hanford, David Saperstein and Jackie Wolcott, for being both my friends and my teachers.

Of course, I could have achieved nothing at all without my staff colleagues at CSW. Every single one of them, past and present, have been talented, committed, passionate and dedicated to serving Christ, one another, and their family around the world. They are an inspiration to me and I thank God for them every day of my life.

Other fellow travellers who do not fall into any of the above categories include my friends at the FCO, Sue Breeze and Margaret Galy, both of whom have provided me with a wealth of knowledge and support for the FORB cause.

Thanks also to those people who have faithfully read, and re-read, some of these chapters to check for factual accuracy and to suggest edits: Sina Adesanya, Jonathan Aitken, Dr Peter Bibawy, Scot Bower, Dr Khataza Gondwe, Emma Howlett, Bill Lowe, Anna-Lee Stangl, and Wael.

Then, of course, a huge thank you to my long term friend, Joel Edwards, who for a very long time pestered and nagged me to actually write this book!

Lastly, and he should have been first, an enormous and heartfelt thanks to Tim Pettingale, who had the courage to take me on as a book project. Tim spent hours and days just listening to me talk about my life, and then had to separate the wheat from the chaff (most of it was chaff), in order to write it all up. He has borne with great fortitude my missed deadlines and constant re-edits, and has produced what I hope you will agree is a readable and interesting book. Thanks Tim, you're a star!

Foreword

Mervyn Thomas has been my friend and prayer partner for over 20 years, so I feel I know him well. When he sent me his autobiography and asked me to write a foreword for it, I opened the book with enthusiasm and anticipation. Merv is a remarkable man and I knew he had a remarkable story to tell.

When I read the full manuscript of *Standing Up, Speaking Out* I felt like echoing the words of the Queen of Sheba on her visit to the Court of King Solomon: *"Behold the half was not told me!"*

For even though I have been Mervyn's confidante, travelling companion to some of the countries where persecution reigns, and his colleague as Honorary President of CSW, I knew less than half of the dramatic and colourful episodes chronicled in these pages.

Because he is by nature such a modest and self-effacing character ("I am a bit of a wimp myself" he erroneously declares at one point in these pages), Mervyn will not thank me for describing him as a hero.

In one sense his modesty is appropriate for, as the chapters of his story unfold, it is clear that the heroism they recount is shared with the staffers and supporters of CSW and above all by the victims whose cause CSW champions.

From Mervyn's CSW casebook there are hair-raising tales of sinister harassment by the Secret Police or *Securitate* under Ceaușescu; of torture testimonies from the brutal regime of North Korea, and of terrifying encounters with armed gangs in Nigeria. Such are the predictable hazards which CSW's victims of persecution regularly have to face.

What CSW has succeeded in doing over the past 40 years, by the excellence of its research and advocacy, is to put its authentic reports of these sufferings high on the agenda of the UN, the US Congress, the British Parliament, the European Parliament and other important agencies and legislatures around the world.

"To be a voice for the voiceless" has been for many years CSW's self-proclaimed mission. It has done and continues to do that job superbly well under Mervyn's leadership.

Mervyn's story is interwoven with generous descriptions of his key friends and allies. High among his co-heroes are the late Stuart Windsor, his memorably unorthodox but brilliantly effective No 2 at CSW, and Congressman Frank Wolf, who has fought the good fight for persecuted minorities in Washington DC in close alliance with Mervyn for many years.

This book is also a family story. It includes a charming account of Mervyn's courtship of his wife Wendy, and a proud paternal pen portrait of his son, Seth (my Godson), who is already proving himself to be a faithful chip off the old block by raising funds for a hospital in the beleaguered Christian village of Asso, Northern Nigeria.

Finally, I should declare an interest in that Mervyn has devoted one of his chapters to his relationship with me. This far too flattering chapter ends with these words: "Without wanting to embarrass him he has been a huge positive influence on my life for the past 25 years in more ways than he'll ever know."

All I can say is that every word in this sentence could just as well have been written by me about Mervyn!

I reciprocate his friendship and his love with prayerful gratitude. Long may Mervyn's Ministry at CSW continue to flourish!

Jonathan Aitken

8 November 2018

Introduction

To say that the staff of the British Embassy in Romania were hostile might be overstating the matter, but they were certainly not pleased to see my colleague and I on their doorstep. A disgruntled Chargé d'affaires had one of his staff escort us to a secure meeting room. It was essentially a concrete bunker in the basement of the embassy – the only room in the entire building they could guarantee was not bugged.

This was the mid-1980's. Romania was in the midst of President Nicolae Ceauşescu's austerity policy – an economic "shock therapy" that would lead to widespread food shortages and a full-blown revolution by 1989. Romania in the 80s had all the hallmarks of North Korea today. It was a Big Brother state and things were pretty bad.

This was my first ever trip to a country where Christians were persecuted. I was accompanied by Justin Fashanu, the footballer, who would become a good friend and, in time, also a member of the board of CSW.

The plan was to rendezvous with CSW colleagues from Switzerland and a group of congressmen from the US. We were all supposed to arrive in Romania at the same time, but I had made a mistake with the dates. Fash and I arrived a couple of days before the Americans. Not knowing quite what to do with ourselves, I thought it would be a sensible idea to visit the embassy and let them know we were in the country.

Sat across the desk from us in the embassy's bunker, the Chargé d'affaires shook his head wearily.

"You can't stay here," he sighed. "You've got to go home. In fact, I don't even know how you managed to get into the country. Your visas were revoked. Whoever let you through passport control is going to be in big trouble."

He then told us that our Swiss colleagues had not travelled, as their visas had been revoked before they left Zurich. As we talked, it became clear that our colleagues from the US Congress were the only ones who were welcome in Romania. Congress was about to vote on a bill that could grant Romania "Most Favoured Nation" trading status – a vital help to its ailing economy. The government wanted to prove to the Americans that all was well in their nation. What they *didn't* want was people like us turning up, causing them difficulties.

"Well, we're here now," I told the Chargé d'affaires. "We're not going home. We'll wait for our American colleagues."

Grudgingly he conceded.

"If you insist. But keep your heads down. Don't get into any trouble. The authorities clearly haven't realised you're here yet."

Returning to our hotel, Fash and I decided to pray and ask God what we should do with the two days we had to kill. But not before Fash had relived one his footballing success stories. He was a big star at the time and somehow – I'll never know how – he had managed to procure an actual football and smuggle it into our hotel room. He then proceeded to re-enact a famous goal he'd scored against Liverpool – smashing the light fitting in the process! After that debacle we had one of the most amazing times of prayer I've ever experienced, and God spoke to me very clearly that we were to go and visit a certain priest in the Romanian Orthodox church.

Father George Calciu had twice been imprisoned by the Romanian authorities, both for long stretches, totalling over 20 years. His was a high-profile case that CSW had been working on, campaigning for his release for a long time. Now out of prison, we had been assured that Father George was free. We were pretty sure, however, that he was actually under house arrest and still very much oppressed. Of course, when the Americans arrived, the authorities would make certain that the house arrest guards vanished for the duration of their visit. But I thought that if we could pre-empt their visit and catch them unawares, we would soon see for ourselves whether or not he was really free.

The only flaw in this plan was that I had no idea where Father George lived. We had no address, no phone number, nothing. On the way to the embassy from the hotel, however, I'd noticed a tiny little church on the main road called the Anglican Church of the Resurrection. I thought that might be a good place to begin making enquiries.

Fash and I found our way to this modest looking building with the minister's small apartment adjoining and knocked on the door. An American priest, Father John Keefers, answered the door.

"Can we come in and speak with you?" I asked.

Hearing my English accent, he became very nervous. Glancing furtively around he ushered us in off the street as quickly as he could. Once inside, he put a single finger to his lips and went to put on some music, turning it up very loud.

"What do you want?" he asked in barely audible whisper.

"Could you turn the music down?" I said.

"No. Everywhere is bugged in this church. And everything is listened to," he told me.

As soon as I said that we intended to visit Father George Calciu and wanted to know where he lived, the colour drained from his face.

"You can't," he said. "Don't even try to go near him. It's too dangerous. Father George is regarded as a high-profile enemy of the State."

"I know, but I believe God has told us to go and visit him," I said.

"He can't have," Father John responded, which raised my eyebrows.

"But do you know his address?" I persisted.

"Yes, I know where he lives."

"Well, will you take us there?"

He shook his head.

"No, no, no! In any case, I have to take a wedding this afternoon."

Not willing to let it go, Fash told him in that case we'd come back after the wedding. Of course, he begged us not to return and hustled us out of his apartment. Undeterred, however, we went back a few hours later and banged on his door again. Clearly, we were the last people he wanted to see, but eventually, reluctantly he agreed to take us "close" to where Father George lived. He was only prepared to drop us several streets away; we'd have to walk the rest.

* * *

Father John pulled over his dilapidated old car wrote down his address and pointed in the direction we should head. He had been agitated for the whole journey and couldn't wait to get going. It has to be said, at this point, that we stood out like a sore thumb, so Father John had just cause for concern. Although Caucasian, I looked and dressed like a foreigner, and there were simply no black men in Romania at that time. Fash wasn't a small man either!

We made our way through the streets towards the apartment block where Father George lived. Much of the housing was contained in communist style, grey monolithic tower blocks. Each resident's address was identified by the confusing (to a foreigner) sequence of a road name, then a block number, followed by a gate number, a row number, and finally a door number. Even armed with this information, it was far from obvious which block was which.

We eventually worked out where we were supposed to be and walked towards one of the blocks. It was a sunny day and there were children playing outside in the street. We saw a group of soldiers gathered together, lounging on the steps outside of the block in question. If we didn't know before, we were now certain we had the right place.

The soldiers were talking loudly, laughing, a couple of them smoking cigarettes, and clearly under the influence of drink. When they spotted us approaching, they all stood up, very much back on duty. Fash and I decided to walk past them, not attempting to enter the block, and stopped at a small park, just beyond. Wondering what our next move should be, we prayed. Although it sounds funny now, at the time the chorus *Be Bold, Be Strong* was popular, so we sang it to each other in the park! Neither of us felt particularly bold or strong. But we decided we were going to turn around and walk up the steps, past the guards, and see what happened.

We managed to climb two steps and were then grabbed by the guards and roughly bundled back onto the pavement. They were intimidating, each carrying an automatic rifle, and none of them able to speak a word of English. After a minute or so of shouting in Romanian and gesticulating to no effect, they shoved a gun in each of our backs and marched us away from the block, back onto the main street.

In the couple of minutes it took to escort us away, half a dozen unmarked cars had screeched to a halt nearby and secret policemen tumbled out of them, like a scene from *Bridge of Spies*. The *Securitate* surrounded us and began to question us. A couple of them could speak English. A tall, grey haired man demanded to know exactly what we were doing.

"We've come to visit a member of our family," I told him.

"Who?" he demanded.

"Father George Calciu," I replied.

Once again, his name provoked a strong reaction. More shouting in Romanian followed.

"He is an enemy of the State," the man barked.

"But I thought he was free?" I responded as innocently as possible.

"What do you want him for?" the tall man asked.

"We just want to pray with him."

"Well you can't."

"Why not? What law is there to say we can't pray with him?" I ventured.

While our frustrating conversation continued, Fash, who truthfully didn't really understand what all the fuss was about, was showing off his state-of-the-art Sony Walkman to some curious secret policeman, letting him listen to his music (which happened to be a cassette of worship songs from the Christian Centre Nottingham). At one point he said,

"If you let us go and pray with our friend, I'll give this to you."

He almost pulled off that deal, but unfortunately that guy wasn't the boss.

The tall man asked me over and again,

"Where is the man who brought you here? What is his name?"

I played dumb. Fash overheard and almost gave the game away,

"Oh, he's…"

"We don't know who he was," I put in hastily. "He was just a friendly stranger who agreed to give us a ride."

I wondered what would happen next. The men began to hustle us towards one of their cars and I thought we would be taken away. But then someone said something in Romanian and, inexplicably, everyone stepped away from us, got back into their vehicles and drove away as quickly as they'd arrived. We were left standing on the street by ourselves, utterly bemused.

By now the soldiers had returned to their post and resumed guard of the tower block. We knew it was fruitless to make another attempt to get into the building, so we made our way back to our hotel via public transport. Despite not being able to see Father George, we felt we'd made our point. We'd let the authorities know that *we knew* he wasn't a free man.

Arriving back at the hotel reception we went to collect our room key and were told, "Ah, Mr Thomas and Mr Fashanu – we have found a better room for you."

"Oh, thanks very much," said Fash.

"No, no," I interrupted, "we're quite happy with the room we have."

It was useless to protest. We were under surveillance. Wherever we went from then on, nine or ten secret police officers went with us, and not very discretely. The *Securitate* watched and followed us everywhere. They were so amateurish we could spot them a mile off. Like every cliché from a bad spy movie, furtive looking men in sunglasses and trench coats peered over the tops of newspapers.

The next day the Americans arrived – congressmen Frank Wolfe, Chris Smith and Tony Hall. We later learned that the first thing the authorities told them was that the two Englishmen would be deported immediately. Frank Wolfe had intervened.

"If you send them home, we go home as well," he said, and refused to budge on the matter. Grudgingly, they were forced to let us stay.

* * *

Although on the face of it, our mission had been frustrated, in fact it was more successful than we knew. Father George had seen us and subsequently heard that we'd tried to visit him. The knowledge that someone had travelled to his country and made an effort to see him encouraged him greatly. Within weeks of us leaving, the authorities set him free, releasing him from house arrest. Father George and I would go on to become great friends.

Numerous similar stories can be told in different parts of the world, in different contexts. Although it might not seem like much to some, showing solidarity with those who are being persecuted – even if it is just making an attempt to visit them, to pray with them – gives them hope. And hope should never be underestimated.

1. Influences

With a name like Mervyn Thomas, most people assume I must be Welsh and, to be honest, I have always supported Wales in any sporting events.

Growing up I would ask my Dad if I had any Welsh roots, and he told me that, according to his dad, our family was from Treorchy in the Rhondda Valley. Just a few years ago I had a conversation with my elderly Aunt Grace (Dad's sister), who informed me that her Dad had told her the family were from Pontypridd – not too far away from Treorchy, and still in the Welsh valleys.

However, it still wasn't 100% clear and we were determined to find out where in Wales our forefathers hailed from. After a great deal of digging, we eventually discovered that my ancestors going back six generations to 1735 were all born in Chatham, Kent. So much for my Welsh heritage. Of course, by marrying a Welsh girl I at least ensured my son was half Welsh!

* * *

My Dad was an old-fashioned kind of father. Syd Thomas was a dad of the 50s. I was born seven years after the end of the Second World War, and dads in that era were not "hands-on" in the way I am with my son, Seth. Dad was strict. Not overbearing, but you knew there were certain things that were non-negotiable.

No doubt he was a product of his own childhood. His father had belonged to the *Peculiar People* – a very strict Christian group who were part of the holiness movement. ("Peculiar" as in set apart, rather than "odd"). Today some might consider them a sect, but they were a kind of cross between Brethren and Pentecostal church streams.

The Peculiar People believed in the infallibility of Scripture and lived very simple lives. Things that most people considered recreation were labelled "out of bounds" – including going to the cinema and football.

My Grandad wasn't allowed to play football because it was considered "sinful". I've no idea why! As a result, he kept a pair of football boots permanently at his friend's house, so he could play secretly at school.

These things carried over into the way my Dad brought up me and my sister, Meg. On a Sunday he wouldn't allow any television, wouldn't buy a newspaper (or anything for that matter), and didn't really like me going outside to play, though he eventually relented on that.

As I grew up in Grays, Essex, in the 1950s, Dad was an accountant at a big cement works, of which there were many in Essex around that time. He worked on the site now occupied by Lakeside shopping mall. Later he retrained and became what was termed an "industrial relations manager" a precursor to a personnel officer or HR manager. He was well respected in his work and he was also an elder of Grays Pentecostal church, part of the Assemblies of God; a church he'd helped to build.

I know Dad was well loved by many, because over the years, on Father's Day, I've posted a picture of him on Facebook, and each time comments have flooded in from people saying what an amazing godly man he was, and how he had influenced them. I respected Dad too. Perhaps the greatest thing about him was that he was the same man at home as he was at church. He was the same with me as he was in the pulpit – and I knew that meant something. There was no hypocrisy. After my sister left home, Dad used the spare bedroom as his study, and I would often walk past the door and see him on his knees praying or reading his Bible.

Dad ran a Sunday afternoon Bible class for many years and it was here that so many people were influenced by him and found a solid foundation for their faith. Sunday was a busy day in our household which began with us all walking to church (we couldn't take the bus, because that would cause us to make the bus driver *work*, and work was banned on the Sabbath, if you follow the logic). It was a few miles away, so we walked there and back in the morning, had our lunch, walked there and back again for afternoon Sunday school, then did the trip once more for the evening service. I wasn't allowed to go out and play with my friends on a Sunday, but you can probably see that I still got plenty of exercise!

When I was older, church activities extended to the Monday night young people's meeting, the Tuesday night Bible study, Thursday night general prayer meeting, and Friday night young people's prayer meeting. Then on a Saturday we would often be off to a church convention somewhere. Everything else fitted around these events.

Meg and Mum

My sister, Meg, is six and a half years older than me and growing up she used to really annoy me! I think I didn't like her when we were small because she was the goodie two shoes and I was the one who was always getting smacked for something.

In those days, old fashioned discipline didn't come under the scrutiny that it does today, and both my parents had their own approach to it. If my mum lost her temper because I was being naughty, she would just lash out. Usually a slap across the back of the head or legs, whichever was the closest. Dad, on the other hand, would make me go into another room and wait for him. Then he would come in and explain to me why he was going to discipline me. Then he would make me bend over and give me several sharp whacks with the slipper. Yes, it hurt quite a lot.

In all my years growing up, however, I can only remember one occasion when Meg was disciplined in this way. She got a slap on her legs and I was so taken with the fact that she'd had a whack instead of me, that I ran around the house after her shouting,

"Did it hurt, Meg? Did It hurt?"

I was just thrilled it wasn't me for once!

I've always been something of a practical joker. When Meg eventually left home to go and study to become a physiotherapist, she would often call home and reverse the charges. In those days the operator would come on the line and say,

"I have a reverse charge call for you. Are you prepared to accept the charges?"

Knowing full well that it was Meg, sometimes I would just say, "No!" and she'd be forced to hang up.

It was usual for people to answer the phone with their number in those days. I still remember ours:

"Hello, Grays Thurrock 72415?"

However, I would regularly pick up the phone and say,

"Belfast 2626?"

The puzzled operator would say,

"Oh, I'm terribly sorry, I seem to have the wrong number!"

I would hear Meg in the background saying,

"No, it's my brother messing around!"

After she'd left home our relationship changed and I actually started to miss her. Eventually, she moved back home and began working in hospitals in east London. Meg is a very spiritual, pastoral person and, like my dad hugely well respected by many.

As a toddler my Mum used to put me on the back of her bike and cycle to her mum's each Thursday, so that I could visit my maternal Nana and Grandad. Mum's dad was a docker and one of the most stubborn men you could care to meet. Nana died when I was nine of motor neurone disease, which no one seemed to know anything about back then.

Mum didn't come from a Christian family. A neighbour offered to take her to Sunday school and that's where she met my dad. Her parents didn't like her going to church, and they initially didn't like it when she later married my father. She too was involved in church ministry alongside dad, faithfully serving as a Sunday School teacher for 25 years. She would also quietly get alongside some of the younger women in the church, often writing them letters of encouragement.

Grandad Harry

While my dad was a big influence on me growing up, both of his parents also made a great impression on me.

I never met my grandad because he died just before I was born, yet he still managed to exert a great influence on me and I guess I hero worshipped him.

Though he grew up in the somewhat claustrophobic environment of the Peculiar People, Herbert Henry Thomas (Harry or H.H. to his friends) kicked against the excesses of the holiness movement. He occasionally attended a Methodist church, but was essentially a Sunday Christian.

I still have the newspaper cutting of Grandad's obituary, which appeared in a national newspaper. He was a pioneer and his chosen field was the world of brass bands. Harry became the chief organiser of the national brass band championships, which were held at the great Crystal Palace, and he was the Secretary of the London and Home Counties Brass Band Association. It was a role he held for 36 years and I have the gold Hunter pocket watch he received when he retired.

He was also a conductor, and an entrepreneur who launched several other brass band related initiatives. He founded a society for brass band conductors that still exists today. He also started his own music publishing business, producing brass band repertoire, and ran a brass instrument repair shop just off Charing Cross Road. The shop is still there today, but is no longer filled with brass.

Brass bands were Harry's passion and he died doing what he loved. He was conducting a band at the Romford festival in 1951, playing a march called *The Old Comrades*, and collapsed mid-performance. He'd had a heart attack and died on the way to hospital. I was born a year later. I have a silver engraved conductor's baton that was presented to him on the very day that he died.

Grandma Lily

The other figure who loomed large in my formative years was Grandma Lily. Growing up, my paternal grandparents lived right next door to us, so Lily was my next door neighbour. She was half Swiss and one of triplets. Her father had been the head waiter at the Grand Hotel in Brighton when she was growing up, and she told me that he used to stand her on a table and try to teach her how to yodel! She had grown up attending an Anglican church, but it was when her family had moved to Grays in Essex that she attended a Pentecostal crusade where she gave her life to Jesus.

I only ever knew Grandma Lily as a widow, but she was my best friend growing up and I spent a lot of time with her. I didn't necessarily recognise it at the time, but looking back I realise how important her presence was. When I was 10 Mum went out to work as well as Dad, and although these days it's normal for both parents to work, back then it was unusual. Also, during the last year before my Nana died with motor neurone disease, Mum spent many long hours looking after her. This meant that sometimes when I returned home from school I would go straight round to my grandma's and often stayed for tea. Each Friday night I would spend the evening with her watching Dr Kildare on the television and she would cook me chips. (I never had fish because I don't like it. I'm a very fussy eater, but that's another story). Lily was also famous for her wonderful jam tarts (which I did eat).

Lily was a tough lady. At the age of 85 she fell down the stairs at church from top to bottom, breaking her wrist and collar bone. She soon recovered and was back to being as busy as ever. At 90 she collapsed with a burst ulcer. She had several blood transfusions at the hospital and the doctors fully expected that she would never come out – or if she did, that she would never eat properly again. But she made a full recovery within days and, as soon as she was out, came round to our house for lunch and ate more than anyone else!

But the thing I remember most about Lily is that I could talk to her about absolutely anything. She hardly ever complained about anything and was always ready to listen. In fact, one of her catch phrases was, "There's a lot of people worse off than me. I've had a great life!" We would talk about all and sundry and I think this was what helped us become so close.

Lily eventually died of a stroke. I was away for the weekend with a group of young people from the church when I heard and rushed back to see her. She was tucked away by herself in a side ward at the hospital. I had been warned by my dad and my aunt that she was unresponsive, so I shouldn't expect her to speak to me or respond at all. Strangely, though, I went into her room, looked at her and said, "Hello Grandma," and she immediately opened her eyes and looked at me. I sat and chatted to her and her eyes never left me.

Lily loved to sing and was in great demand singing solos at various church's women's meetings. She had a quiet spirituality about her, and was never one to stand at the front of the church giving her testimony or anything like that, But I knew she had a firm faith and that it was very important to her. In her quiet, strong way, she influenced my own faith a great deal.

2. Mischief

When I was primary school age, a new family moved into the area and started coming along to church. Their daughter joined my school and I saw her around the place from time to time. Mum and Dad invited the whole family round for supper one Sunday after church, as was the tradition, and conversation ensued.

"Jenny goes to the same school as Mervyn," said the girl's mum.

"That's nice," said my mum. Turning to Jenny, she asked,

"Have you seen Mervyn at school?"

"Oh yes," Jenny replied sweetly. "I had to go into his class on Wednesday and I saw him standing in the corner."

This "news" was greeted with pursed lips and a cold stare, but nothing was said … not until later.

This incident more or less sums up my school days. I disliked school intensely and I was naughty. "Mischievous" naughty rather than "bad" naughty. But it meant I was often in hot water.

Mum had a brother called Richard. I loved Uncle Dick. He must have been one of the world's biggest practical jokers and I learned a lot from him. It sounds childish (because it is), but if we were in his car, he would constantly beep his horn and wave at pedestrians, who more often than not would wave back with puzzled expressions. It's a family tradition I've kept up to this day!

Some of my practical jokes were on a much grander scale, however. Uncle Eddie Salmon (not my real uncle this time) was the church Sunday school superintendent. He owned a hardware store in Grays bearing his name. Friday was the day when he went up to London and bought all his supplies, and I liked nothing better than to go with him. Supplies were bought from a warehouse in east London, where

Uncle Eddie would go and purchase twenty brooms at a time along with miscellaneous other hardware items. I enjoyed going along for the ride and exploring the cavernous warehouse.

One day we were driving through London and I saw some huge graffiti on the side of a building. Someone had drawn the CND peace symbol and underneath had inscribed the words "Ban the Bloody Bomb". I had no idea what any of this meant – I didn't even know the word "bloody" was classified as swearing – but the image and words stuck in my head.

In my last year at primary school we went on a school trip to a chalk quarry. The point of the trip was to look for fossils. I didn't find any fossils, but I did find a big lump of chalk that I put in my pocket. We returned to school later that day, collected our things, and were dismissed for the day.

Like most schools on a main road, we had a patrol man, Mr South, who would see people safely across the road. Conveniently, Mr South lived more or less opposite the school. His house was on a corner, which meant that he had a long wall that stretched all the way down the side of his house. I contemplated this large "empty canvas" and remembered the chalk in my pocket. On impulse, I wrote "Ban the Bloody Bomb" in huge letters on his wall, then casually walked home, thinking nothing more of it.

Believe it or not, I had more or less forgotten about the whole incident until the next morning in Assembly, when I spotted Mr South standing at the back of the school hall.

"What's he doing in Assembly?" I thought. "He's never come in here before."

Only then did the penny drop.

Our Welsh headmaster, Mr Jenkins, was a very strict, stern-faced man.

He stood up and addressed the school.

"Right, pay attention. Yesterday, someone wrote a slogan on Mr South's wall. You know who you are, so there's no point pretending. Put your hand up and own up now."

Silence.

"Come on, who was it?"

My heart was pounding. *"Oh no, what have I done?"*

There was no way I was putting my hand up.

After several long, uncomfortable silences and repeated requests no one was forthcoming, and the Assembly had to be dismissed. We all went to our respective classes, but the inquisition wasn't over yet.

Our teacher had barely finished taking the register when Mr Jenkins came into our class. He glared at each of us in turn.

"Look, I know the culprit is in this class," he informed us, "because you all went to the chalk quarry yesterday. I'm not leaving this classroom until somebody owns up to writing that graffiti."

As my stomach churned with dread, suddenly one of the other boys, John Cook, stuck up his hand. Cook was a big lad, twice my size, and the school's star goalkeeper and captain of the football team. For one glorious second I thought he was going to take the rap for something he didn't do, just so we could all move on with our lives.

"Please sir," he said, "Mervyn Thomas did it!"

I had recently had something good happen to me: the school had both prefects and monitors, the prefects being the more senior. I had been selected for the post of head monitor at lunchtimes. Since I had now committed a "crime", it was fitting that I be disciplined in a manner befitting someone who had been entrusted with such great responsibility.

It was a bit like being court-martialled. The headmaster gave me the slipper – I was expecting that. But then I was made to stand in front of Assembly the next morning, where I was summarily "de-badged" and disgraced. Of course, I was also equipped with a bucket of water and a brush and made to scrub the wall clean. Finally, I was banned from participating in my favourite activity for a while – sport. I hated most academic lessons at school (especially maths), but I loved sport, even though I never excelled at it. I was detained in the library for several sports lessons and made to do maths.

Despite all of this, the thing I was most terrified of was my dad finding out what had happened. I knew I would end up being punished twice for the offence, and I didn't want to incur my dad's wrath. Astonishingly, the school didn't inform my parents about what I'd done and, for a long while, I thought I'd gotten away with it.

That is, until the results of the Eleven Plus examination came out. I'd only ever been an average student at school and after sitting the Eleven Plus, I was pretty certain that I'd failed it. The day the results came out, one or two of the kids at school whose postman came early had learned of their result before coming to school. One of my mates said,

"Yeah, I'm on the borderline."

The "borderline" was a narrow miss. A fail, but only just. I thought to myself, "I'd like to be on the borderline." For me, the borderline was aspirational!

When I got home that evening I found out that I was indeed on the borderline, but that turned out to be my undoing. There was a process for those who'd missed out by a few marks. Your paper was re-marked and the headmaster had to write an accompanying report on your academic progress and behaviour. The problem was, my mum had to go into the school to talk through the process with Mr Jenkins – a meeting I had to attend. It was at that point that Mr Jenkins spilled the beans on the graffiti.

"Please don't tell Dad!" I pleaded with Mum as we left the meeting. I probably said those four words to her more than any others for the whole of my childhood. Dad would be out at a church prayer meeting, or something similar, and I would be at home, having done something naughty.

"Please don't tell Dad!"

Mum was usually a much softer touch than Dad and on this occasion she decided to show mercy.

Miraculously, with a re-marked paper and the headmaster's report, I passed the Eleven Plus. This was great news for me, because it meant I could go to the school I'd always wanted to go to: Grays County Technical High School – or Grays Tech as it was commonly known.

The grounds of the high school actually backed onto our house. At the bottom of our garden were some railings and as a little boy I would be down there constantly, watching the groundsman, whose name was Bill, mark out the cricket pitch and do other tasks around the sports field.

Some older boys I was friendly with went to the Tech, which was one reason I wanted to go there. The other reason was its proximity to home. All I needed to do was roll out of bed and it took minutes to walk to school.

Not long after I'd joined the school I had a strange incident where I was sleepwalking. I thought I was dreaming everything, but I actually got out of bed and walked out of our front door in my pyjamas and bare feet. I always took the shortcut to school – a narrow gravel path at the end of our road. I hurried down that path thinking to myself, "Wow, this must be hurting my feet," though I couldn't feel anything at the time. I arrived at the school gates and was alarmed to find them locked up (it was 1.00am!).

"Oh no," I thought, "I'm going to be late for my maths lesson!"

I knew that Bill the groundsman lived opposite the school, so I thought, "I know, I'll go and knock on Bill's door and he can open the gate!" As I was banging on his front door, I suddenly woke up and realised that I wasn't in a dream – this was real.

Thankfully, he didn't come to answer the door and I scurried away. Walking home I realised that my feet were covered with cuts from the gravel path. I turned into our road and a person in a car pulled over to ask if I was alright.

"I'm fine, I'm just going home," I replied, as if I routinely went for a walk in my pyjamas in the middle of the night.

Just a couple of hundred yards from home I saw the familiar outline of a person walking towards me. It was Dad. He'd woken up when he heard the front door slam. He looked out of the window and saw me running down the path. "He's going to school!" he'd said to my mum, because of the way I'd taken off, like I did every morning. He quickly got dressed and went out to look for me.

After that night, my parents would leave all sorts of things in our hallway at night – obstacles to make it more difficult for a sleepwalking boy to get to the front door. But I never went sleepwalking again; it was a one off event.

At school I was never the brightest, but not the worst either. I ended up with five O-levels, including English and Maths. As you know, I despised maths. Before sitting our O-levels, we did the customary mock exam papers and our teacher read out everyone's results to the class in descending order of percentage.

"Smith, 87%. Wilson, 85%..." etc.

This continued for some time and my name wasn't read out.

"Jones, 20%. Ward, 18%..."

"Surely, I can't have done this badly?" I thought.

"Thomas, 4%."

After that dire result, six months later I miraculously passed my maths O-level. The main reason for this was that Grandma Lily took in a lodger. The lodger turned out to be the headmaster of another local school, whose job it was to mark maths papers. He sat me down and showed me how he marked each question, explaining things as he went along.

"It's not just about getting the right answer," he informed me, "it's about the workings out as well."

He pointed out things that I hadn't got from my usual maths teacher and it did the trick.

I remained the mischievous Mervyn Thomas I'd been at primary school, however, and was constantly on the edge of getting into trouble. On the last day of school before we broke up for the Christmas holidays, someone dared me to jump out of the hall window, mid-Assembly, so I did.

A teacher was busy speaking at the front and I was sitting near the open window. Suddenly I just stood up and leapt out of the window into the quad. (It wasn't very high!) Then I walked around the side of the school and casually came back in via the main entrance.

Everyone was starting to come out of Assembly, and I was confronted by Bill the groundsman, who appeared from nowhere. The timing of the events in the next few seconds were unfortunate, to say the least. Bill stopped me and spoke just as the headmaster was walking past to go into his office.

"I saw you jump out of the hall window!" Bill said.

The headmaster stopped in his tracks.

"He did what?!"

I was ushered straight into his office.

"I don't want to have to punish you just before Christmas, Thomas," the headmaster said, "but I don't have a choice."

He gave me six of the best with the cane on my hand, which I assure you hurt a great deal. He had a special, deadly technique for this, which involved striking "through" your outstretched palm, then bringing his cane back at such an angle that he whacked your knuckles with the up stroke. It was effectively twelve of the best.

Then there was the "biology lab incident". I can't remember my biology teacher's proper name, because we all referred to her as "Lulu". There is an unwritten rule that all the naughty boys in a class must sit together at the back. Several of us were sat on the bench seat and we'd noticed there was a trap door in the floor. Someone dared me to go down the trap door when Lulu wasn't looking and, when she turned around to write on the board, I hopped in. Of course, my mates thought it was incredibly funny to move their chairs on top of the trap door, so that I couldn't get back out!

There was a surprisingly large cavity underneath the classroom floor, but it was incredibly dusty, with cobwebs, and contained a network of pipes. I knocked on the floor above my head – not too loudly, as I didn't want the teacher to discover what I'd done – but to no avail. I moved around a bit to see if there was another way of escaping and became a bit disorientated. After a minute or so of clambering around I spotted a square of light. "There's the trap door," I thought. "I'll give it a good, hard shove and get out of here!"

What I didn't realise was that I'd crawled the whole length of the lab and there was another trap door, right in front of the teacher's chair.

She'd just finished writing on the board and turned around to address the class when the trap door under her desk flew open and out I popped! I remember her screaming,

"Thomas!!!"

I didn't get the cane for that misdemeanour, but I did get a detention.

Mr Batt was the senior master in the school, number two to the headmaster, and known for being exceptionally strict. He was also very particular about the use of the English language and would frequently pull students up on their grammar. I saw him play out the following scenario numerous times.

We would be in his class, held in a room that was another class's form room. A junior boy would knock on the door, mid-lesson, needing something from his desk he'd forgotten to take with him.

"Please sir, can I get my English book?"

We knew what was coming.

"Yes, of course you *can*. Where is it?"

"In my desk sir."

"Well, of course, you *can* go and get it."

(The junior boy heads towards his desk).

Batt, shouting: "Hey! Where do you think you are going?"

Startled boy: "To get my book sir."

"Well, I haven't given you my permission!"

"What do you mean sir?"

"Ask my permission!"

"Err, can I go and get my book sir?"

"Yes, of course, you *can* go and get your book..."

This went on for some time until Batt eventually explained that "can" just means you are capable of retrieving your English book. "May I get my English book?" is the correct term.

My best mate at school was "Ears" Barker, known to many as "Flappers". You'll have guessed that he had huge ears. His real name was Ian. Strangely enough, it was Ears who got me interested in the world of brass bands – despite my dad and grandad's involvement in that world. Ears played a baritone. Those uninitiated in brass band culture will often say, "A baritone what?" but it's just called a baritone – a sort of cross between a euphonium and a tenor horn. Grandma Lily gave me a very old battered cornet that was sitting in her shed which had belonged to my grandad, and I learned to play it fairly badly.

Ears decided it would be good if I accompanied him to the Grays Temperance Silver Prize Band Hall to meet the bandmaster, Ernie Merrick. I knew that name – I'd heard my dad mention Ernie. They had played together in a band and had pretty much grown up together. Ears took me to meet him. Ernie said,

"If you want to join the band it's sixpence per week and you have to pay now."

"OK, that's fine," I said.

"What do you want to play then?" he asked.

"Baritone please," I said, "because that's what my grandad used to play."

"Oh yes? So who was your grandad?"

"H.H. Thomas," I told him.

"Your grandad was Harry Thomas?!" he said in awe. "In that case, you don't have to pay anything. You can join for nothing because Harry Thomas taught me everything I know."

So I joined Grays Temperance band, but I was pretty rubbish because I never practised! I used to love it when we played for the Remembrance service at the Grays War Memorial, however. My grandad had survived the First World War. He was in the trenches in Belgium and everyone was blown up around him, but somehow he survived. I still have his medals at home – he was a Sergeant in the King's Royal Rifles. So the chance to honour him and countless other soldiers was not to be missed.

Ears' Barker's mum used to go to a local Baptist church and I invited Ears to come to our church's young people's meetings from time to time. He came to several and there was a chorus at the time that went, "Jesus is wonderful, Jesus is mine; He is the one that I love". One day at school, right in the middle of our technical drawing mock exam, Ears was obviously bored and suddenly, from the back of the class, his voice boomed out, "Jesus is wonderful, Jesus is mine; He is the one that I love!"

That was Ears all over. He was as much a practical joker as me. One of his tricks for getting out of lessons was to say he felt unwell, then he'd rush to the cloakroom. There he would chuck a bag of broken biscuits, brought specially for the occasion, into the sink and run water over them, to make it look as though he'd been sick, at which point he'd be sent home. I tried to copy his technique one time, but was caught emptying the biscuits into the sink by the PE master!

For the last three years at Grays Tech, I took a subject called Economic and Public Affairs. As boring as this sounds, I found it really fascinating. It was a mixture of economics and the workings of the British constitutional system. You could take it for O-level, so I did. I remember getting 99% in my mock exam and being hauled before my teacher who insisted that I must have cheated. I hadn't though – it was just a subject that I was interested in and, of course, a sign of things to come.

3. Turning Points

Both the quiet spirituality of my Grandma Lily, and the rock solid consistency of my dad's faith, had an effect on my own. Ultimately, however, faith is something you need to discover for yourself. Several turning points led to my faith being cemented and helped me to realise that I wanted to do something useful with my life; to connect with God's purpose for me and make the most of every opportunity He gave me.

I'd attended Sunday school classes for years and Mum and Dad had always told me about faith in Jesus. I'd even come top of the District in the annual Scripture Union exam, but sometimes it takes other people or events for those words of truth to hit home. I'd put up my hand lots of times in Sunday School over the years, whenever there was a call to receive Jesus, but I didn't really understand what I was doing. Often we would have groups of students visiting the church from the Assemblies of God Bible College at Kenley in Surrey, and it was on one of those occasions that I responded to the altar call and knew in my heart that it was real. That day, Cliff Beasley, one of the students who I got to know quite well over the years, explained the Gospel in a way that really connected with me. I was nine years old.

I got baptised in water two years later, but then a year after that when I was twelve our church was visited by the minister Richard Bolt, and we had a series of healing meetings. Richard was an Anglican minister who had come into a supernatural ministry of the Holy Spirit. He was a fascinating character, not just because he was one of the early Charismatic Anglicans, but also because he was quite an eccentric character. My dad had asked him to come because we didn't have a permanent pastor at the time, so, for a couple of weeks, meetings were held every night and people came for prayer for healing. We saw many amazing miracles take place.

It was a big deal in Grays and the meetings were advertised on the local buses. So many people came to the meetings that we had to get creative about how to deal with the crowds. We managed to rig up a closed circuit TV system, so that people gathered in the basement could follow the meeting – something that's commonplace nowadays, but was really thinking outside the box at the beginning of the sixties.

During an after-meeting with the young people Bolt asked,

"If there is anyone here who hasn't yet received the baptism of the Holy Spirit, put your hand up."

I put my hand up straightaway. The next thing I knew he'd placed his hand on my head and "bam", I experienced the Holy Spirit hitting me like a wave, and spontaneously began speaking in tongues. It was an amazing experience and afterwards everything seemed different about my spiritual life – like I'd gone from black and white to colour.

The following year, as I turned 13, we found a new pastor for the church, who would turn out to be another influential figure. Harold Young was an amazing character. He had come from Bishop Auckland, where his dad had been known as a notorious drunkard. However, this hardened alcoholic had been healed and saved and, as a result, all four of his sons had gone into the ministry. Harold lived with us for a time and became like a second dad to me. He started up a regular Friday night prayer meeting for the youth. Our young people met in a small room in the church and, the meetings were full on, with us all kneeling, and many manifestations of the Holy Spirit.

Our regular Youth meetings on a Wednesday night were held in the church basement, which was accessible from outside the building and the entrance was opposite a café. For a period of time, this café attracted a bunch of characters the locals considered "undesirable" – a chapter of Hell's Angels. Someone from the church made a point of inviting them, however, and some of them turned up to our youth meetings.

Not long before this, someone had received a prophetic word about God bringing people into the church and said we would "hear the sound of them coming". It was interesting, therefore, that on these nights we'd hear the sound of motorbikes outside, followed by the sound of their heavy biker boots coming down the stone stairs to the basement. Everyone felt that was significant.

I was a bit timid around these characters, but we did begin to build a relationship with them. There was no denying the clash of cultures though. One of the more serious young ladies used to play the piano for our choruses. On one occasion, for a joke, literally mid-chorus, one of the bikers suddenly produced a dead cat from his jacket, lifted the piano lid and stuffed it inside. Of course, this put an end to the chorus and the lady fled in tears.

In the following months, the attendance of the Hell's Angels tailed off, but one of the guys (not the dead cat prankster), Richard Earl, kept on coming and gave his heart to the Lord. Later he went to Bible college, got married and became a church pastor. It impressed me how God can take someone He's chosen for His purposes, pluck them out of a completely different culture, and just transform them.

Wilderness years

Despite all my experiences, I still went through some wilderness years in my late teens. Like all kids, I suppose it was my rebellious period. I never did anything really wild, but my walk with God had become distant and I'd started smoking. I'd also developed a habit of swearing and I was hanging around with some people who weren't doing me any good.

Each year our church would attend the East Ham convention, which was a massive gathering of Pentecostals. It happened at Easter so we called it the Easter-Ham convention! One year the speaker was a man called John Whitfield Foster, who was an amazing preacher. I went along as normal, but knew that I wasn't where I should be with the Lord. We began singing a typical old Pentecostal chorus, which usually went on for half an hour. It was nothing special, yet I experienced God's presence in a fresh way. I came away from that weekend feeling so much closer to God, but truthfully my life was still drifting. Then an incident happened that shocked me back to reality.

At one point, I had been a Sunday School teacher at the church. My dad was actually against me doing it, because I was older and he wanted me to attend the Bible class he was running. People tended to "graduate" from Sunday School to Bible class in our church, but they were desperately short of teachers and I wanted to do it. During this time, two brothers went through my class, Andrew and Sydney Barbour. Their parents had emigrated from the West Indies. These lads were absolute terrors, but loveable terrors, and I grew close to them.

Years later, when the boys had grown up, I bumped into Sydney in the street. I was around twenty and at that time I was still not where I should have been with God. The only reason I'd not stopped going to church was out of respect for my dad, knowing how upset he would be. I never lost my faith, but I wasn't living how I should have been. Sydney and I chatted.

"I haven't seen you at church for ages," I told him.

"No, it's not for me," Sydney replied.

"But what about all those years where we learnt from the Bible together?" I asked him.

"Yeah, but you taught us all that stuff from the Bible," he said, "then I heard you swearing and shouting round the back of the Conservative Club, and I thought, what a hypocrite!"

I was stunned by this and suddenly the double life I'd been leading was laid bare.

To make matters worse, a couple of years later I heard that Sydney had been killed. He had a small sports car and for some reason he'd pulled onto the hard shoulder while driving round the M25. While he was parked there a lorry ploughed into the back of him, killing him instantly.

I was so fond of Sydney and his brother. Hearing of his death, I just couldn't shake the conversation we'd had from my mind. I felt guilty about it for a long time. But this incident brought me to my senses and marked the start of me wanting to pursue God's purpose for my life with everything I had. I knew I couldn't continue living the way I had been. I knew that God had a specific purpose for my life. I just needed to find out what it was.

4. Work and Politics

For a long while, the only job I wanted was to be a lorry driver. The transport manager at Tunnel Cement, where my dad worked as Industrial Relations Manager, used to give him large black and white photographs of the lorries, which he would bring home and give to me. I thought they were amazing looking machines and I could think of nothing better than driving one of those around all day, shifting loads of cement.

I suspected though, that if I told my dad I wanted to be a lorry driver he'd say,

"No, son, you want to do better than that."

Not that there is anything wrong with driving a lorry, but I knew my dad, so I told him I wanted to be a transport manager. He spoke to his work colleague who said the best way was to learn everything there was to know about the vehicles themselves to begin with, so an engineering apprenticeship with a lorry manufacturer was a good place to start.

For a while that was the plan, but deep down I couldn't see myself doing an apprenticeship – I am, and always have been, absolutely useless doing anything with my hands! Then one day we were on a family holiday in Matlock in Derbyshire, and I told my parents,

"I know what I want to do. I want to go and work in a bank."

Truth be told, I didn't really *want* to go and work in a bank, but I'd chatted to the careers officer at school and it transpired that you needed five O-levels to get into banking, including Maths and English. I was hoping to get five O-levels, so it just seemed a fairly easy option.

The closure of my school was the deciding factor. I'd thought about staying on at school to do a couple of A-levels, but then it was closed down to be rebuilt over the following two years and reopened as a comprehensive. This meant that to study A-levels I'd have to travel to another school five miles away. Rather than do that, I made up my mind to leave.

Around this time Dad went on a training course and met someone who happened to be the district personnel manager for the Westminster bank in Chelmsford. I don't' know whether my dad had any influence, but I applied to several banks and was offered two jobs, one of which was at Westminster bank.

I started work as a junior clerk at our local branch in Grays High Street. Despite now being grown up with a "proper job", unfortunately this didn't deter my penchant for practical jokes. One of the worst pranks I committed during my time there was to hide £20,000 then forget that I'd done it!

I was a cashier by this time. The chief cashier was a bit of a dreamer and often wasn't paying attention to what he was doing. One day he counted out £20,000 in £5 notes, put the money into plastic bags and sealed them. Protocol dictated that the money was to be put immediately into the safe. He, however, left it sitting on his chair while he went off to make a cup of tea.

I saw these bags of money sitting there and, on impulse, thought I would teach him a lesson. I picked them up and hid them in a cupboard that held one of the large bank ledgers we used. I anticipated chaos breaking out when he returned with his cup of tea – "Oh no! Where's the money gone?" – at which point I'd put him out of his misery. But he was such a dreamer that he just sat down at his desk and carried on working as if nothing had happened! I carried on with my work and thought, "He'll realise eventually" and, believe it or not, I then forgot all about the incident.

We got to the end of the day, however, and it was time to cash up. Lo and behold, the chief cashier was £20,000 short. Even then, unbelievably I didn't remember what I'd done.

In those days the bank used to close at 3.00pm. At 6.00pm we were all still there, with the bank manager. Everyone was checking every single transaction the bank had carried out that day. £20,000 short didn't necessarily mean it was cash – it may have been a combination of many different transactions.

But after three hours the money still hadn't been found and eventually the manager said,

"That's it, I'm locking down the bank and calling in the inspectors, and everyone will have to stay here until this is sorted."

Then, turning to me, he said,

"Thomas, you put all the ledgers away while we're waiting."

As I did so, of course I came across the hidden money!

"Oh!" I piped up. "Look at this!"

Everyone was so relieved that the money had turned up, especially the manager, that there was no inquest to discover how it had gotten there. A narrow escape!

But then, the world of banking was very different in the 70s to today. Here's just one example of the sort of thing that would happen.

Two years after I began work at Westminster bank it changed its name to NatWest and I moved to a larger branch. I was hoping to get into the personnel side of banking to do the same kind of work as my dad.

We managed a sub-branch of the bank which was based inside the Mobil Oil Refinery in Essex. It was my job to run this branch each day and make sure they had everything they needed. Often, I had small amounts of cash to transport there or back in my minivan, and I always travelled with a bank security guard. My "guard" was George Willson, who was in his seventies, and he would always make me stop at a newsagent along the route, so he could buy some cigarettes.

The oil refinery had hundreds of employees who would want to cash their pay cheques on a weekly basis, so we needed to hold a lot of cash on site. Usually, this was delivered by Securicor at the beginning of each week, but on one particular Monday morning they delivered the money to our main branch office by mistake.

The manager said to me,

"OK, Thomas, just take that money with you when you go down there."

George and I set off, only this time with £60,000 in cash in my minivan – a lot of money in the early 70s. As usual, George wanted to stop at the newsagent and buy his cigarettes and I decided to buy a newspaper, so I went in with him. I didn't realise until we got back that I hadn't even bothered to lock my car. Fortunately, the money was still sitting there. Thinking back, the bank manager never even asked me to call and let him know I'd arrived safely. I could have absconded and been out of the country within a couple of hours!

* * *

Every couple of months at church, the young people would take the evening service, which meant that one of us would deliver the main message, one would lead the meeting and so on. The church culture was such that the pastor would just drop on you and say, "Mervyn, come up and give a testimony," so I was used to having to speak in public. Leading the service meant someone had to announce the next hymn, or say a prayer, or give a short testimony, and though I was the youngest in our youth group, I seemed to be the go-to person for this and I really enjoyed it.

When the bank sent me on a management development course that included some public speaking, I was in my element. Because I'd started work at the bank as a 16-year old I'd missed out on some training. There was a pathway for those who came into the bank after completing their A-levels, and there was a clear graduate training programme, but neither was applicable to me.

Eventually, however, the bank manager sent me on a First Development course the bank had recently launched, and I was one of the youngest ever to do it. The majority of the other people on the course were graduates who'd been at the bank for a while.

On two occasions we were required to give a public speech of some kind. Not everyone is suited to this kind of thing and it filled some of the participants with terror, but I felt completely relaxed – which I put down to my experience in church. The course leader told me I was by far the best public speaker he'd ever had on the course.

Midway through the 70s I was seconded to work in the Southend-on-Sea area office. While I was there, a banking personnel job was advertised for the regional office. There were about fifteen area offices which made up the south east region, so moving up to regional banking was a big thing; a real step up. I applied for the job and got it, and spent the next four years as assistant to the regional personnel manager – a job I absolutely loved.

There were about half a dozen NatWest regions across the UK, and each year every region was allowed to nominate one employee for the prestigious Chief Executive's Award. If you won it, you were allowed to travel anywhere in the world you wanted for a month, to study anything you chose, all expenses paid. The only condition was that you had to write a 10,000 word essay on your chosen topic.

It was the head of the bank's way of giving an incentive to the workforce and developing young people, giving them a wider perspective. There were two reasons why you might win the award: for being outstanding at your job, or for outstanding public service. Several people in our office had mentioned they thought I should get the award for my involvement in the community.

I was still active with our local church, but I had also become involved with the local Conservative group. One of the regular bank customers I dealt with was Graham Bright (now Sir Graham Bright) and we often chatted. Graham told me about the Young Conservatives group and I thought I would check it out. I ended up becoming quite involved, helping out with election administration and eventually as treasurer. I was also a Governor of my old primary school, and yes Mr Jenkins was still Headmaster!

I didn't think I had any chance of getting the award, however. There were fifteen areas in our region, with eight thousand employees. Added to that, it was my boss who had to choose the recipient, and he was the type of guy who wanted to be seen to be doing the right thing, so I assumed that ruled me out; he wouldn't want to nominate one of his direct staff.

Nevertheless, my name was put forward and I got the award. It was a dream come true because I got to travel to America for a month and my chosen area of study was Christian TV and radio. Every Friday night I listened to the programme *It's Revival Time* which was broadcast on Radio Luxembourg, so I was interested to find out more about how that kind of programme was made. Remember, in the 70's neither Christian TV or radio was permitted in the UK. My old pastor, Harold Young, had preached all over the US, so he was able to give me some contacts.

I began my trip by flying out to Chicago, then went to visit the Assemblies of God headquarters in Springfield, Missouri, because they had a large radio department. Then I visited Dallas, Phoenix and Tucson. (I only visited Tucson because I was a fan of cowboy movies and it seemed like an iconic place to visit!) I ended the trip by visiting San Francisco to meet Rev Paul Schoch, who was a regular speaker at Assemblies of God conferences and had his own TV station.

As well as being the pastor of a large church and running his TV station, Paul Schoch also taught at the Assemblies of God Bible school in California, and he encouraged me to give up what I was doing and come and study at the Bible College. The people I'd met in Springfield had encouraged me to do the same thing.

This offer helped me to clarify what I felt I should be doing with my life. I realised that Bible College, and a life in academia, just wasn't really for me. I didn't feel any sense that God was calling me to it. I returned home from this trip and immersed myself in the local Conservative party, and before long I was asked if I would be willing to stand as a candidate in the local council elections. I prayed about it for a long time and became convinced that God was calling me into politics. But not before I'd had a major wobble.

I didn't know too much about politics. All I'd heard were the rather left-wing views of the teacher who'd taken us for Economics and Public Affairs at school. We lived in a staunch Labour area in Grays, but my dad was strongly Conservative in his political views, and we had many debates about the different parties' perspectives.

I remember when I went out to play football at lunchtime at school, it would be Labour vs Conservative! Even at the age of 10 it's amazing how the politics of everyone's parents had filtered down to that level. (The Labour team had about 25 kids to choose from, compared to the four of us Conservatives, which spoke volumes about the area!)

After my trip to the States I'd gone back to working in branch banking and immersed myself working with the local Conservative party. I got involved in lots of different aspects of the party and it became something of an obsession, to the detriment of my involvement with the church. Then the party began suggesting that I stand for local election. I was only 23, and I knew it would be quite a coup if I got in.

I had lots of chats with my dad about it. He was very supportive of what I wanted to do, but along with others was concerned that it was pulling me away from church. I managed to convince him that it was a good thing for Christians to be involved with politics. If I'm really honest, though, initially I was doing it for egotistical reasons. I wanted to see my name up in lights! But it really wasn't the done thing for a Pentecostal in those days. A Christian's role was to preach the Gospel and nothing else – especially not getting involved in the dirty world of politics. Nobody thought that you could be preaching the Gospel by being involved in public life. I remember writing an article in the Assemblies of God magazine, *Redemption Tidings*, entitled "We need Pentecostal Politicians". It didn't go down too well!

However, I agreed to stand, but it was just a couple of months before the elections when I had my crisis about what I really wanted to do. I wondered if I'd been wrong to decide against going to Bible college, and thought maybe I should go after all. I came to a decision: yes, I should go to Bible college, which meant I needed to tell my employers, the bank, that I intended to leave, and also tell the local Tory party that I wouldn't be standing for election after all.

The Tories took this news very badly. They said I had badly let them down and they totally cut me off. I left the party for a couple of years and had very little to do with them, because I was like an outcast. Having just won the Chief Executive's Award, my colleagues at the bank also couldn't believe that I was now going to throw in my banking career to go off to Bible college. I didn't have a leaving date at that point, but I'd told them it was a matter of time before I'd leave to go to the US.

Having informed everyone of my decision, I wrote to the contacts I'd made in the States. First, I wrote a letter to the Assemblies of God college in Springfield, Missouri. After several weeks I'd heard nothing back, so I decided to write to Paul Schoch in San Francisco. Several weeks went by with no response, so I wrote again. And again, several weeks after that. To my dismay it seemed as though God was closing that door after all, and I had burned my bridges.

"What's going on God?" I prayed. "I've put my banking career on hold and it looks like I'm not going into politics, so now what?"

Interestingly, I bumped into Paul Shoch at the Assemblies of God conference the following year and got an opportunity to speak to him. I told him I'd written to him three times and never heard back and he insisted he'd never received my letters, so I knew God was up to something.

In 1977 a local Labour councillor who had also been mayor died, so there was going to be a by-election. I was walking down Grays High Street one day when I bumped into one of my old Conservative party colleagues. If I had to bump into anyone, it was ironic it was him, because he was one of the people I'd upset the most by deciding not to stand and, politically, we didn't really see eye to eye on many things! Nevertheless, he stopped me for a chat.

"Oh Merv, how are you? Did you hear about Roy dying? Have you thought about standing?"

I could hardly believe my ears. This was the last person I thought would encourage me back into politics.

I had prayed a lot about things and said to God, "Lord, for whatever reason you've closed the door to Bible college. If you want me to be involved in politics after all, you're going to have to open the door."

This was as clear an open door as I was going to get, and this time I felt ready for it. It was no longer about me and my ego, but a chance to serve my community if that's what God wanted me to do.

"Yes, I'll consider doing it," I told him.

To cut a long story short, I stood for election, and even though Grays was a safe Labour seat, with a Labour government in power, I was elected, beating a hard-headed Scottish union rep, aptly named Jimmy Aberdeen.

The council were pretty upset. The vast majority of councillors were Labour with only three or four Conservatives, and to make matters worse here was this 24-year old upstart. At my first council meeting, rather than putting me with the other Conservatives, they made sure I sat in the place previously occupied by the guy who had died, right in the middle of all the Labour councillors. I wondered at first if God really knew what He was doing, but as things turned out, I got to know those Labour councillors well, and often liked them better than some of my Conservative colleagues.

Over the years I fought three election campaigns and gradually saw the council become more balanced between Conservative and Labour, until in 1981 an administration was formed with a coalition of Conservatives and a range of independents – our coalition had a majority of one!

Each year I attended the Conservative party conference in Blackpool and one year met a guy called David Atkinson. He had just been chosen as parliamentary candidate for Bournemouth East in a by-election. I got to know him because he was originally from Essex and knew Graham Bright. David would turn out to be an important figure in CSW in years to come.

* * *

I eventually left banking altogether when my dad spotted a job advert for an assistant personnel officer at Thames Board Mills in Purfleet. It was a Unilever company that manufactured cardboard, based not far from my dad's work at Tunnel Cement, and it felt right to apply for it.

In those days, of course, people tended to have a single career they stuck with throughout their life, whereas today it's not uncommon for people to have several careers throughout their working life. I remember my mum being unhappy about me leaving the bank for that reason, but dad encouraged me to apply and I got the job.

I worked at Thames Board Mills for five years and eventually became the Mill Personnel Officer. This was during an era where everything revolved around the trade unions. It often seemed that the most powerful people in the mill were not the management, but by far the union reps, who belonged to SOGAT. I'll never forget my first day working there.

I arrived and was directed to the office I would be sharing with the two clerks who would be working for me, the assistant personnel manager. Stuck to the door of the office was a picture of me – the one I'd used when campaigning for local election – with a pin stuck in me and some obscenity scrawled underneath. It sent a pretty clear message: *you're not welcome here!*

Within six months I had managed to win people over and got along with everyone really well. In fact, to this day I still exchange Christmas cards with the senior union rep from those Mill days. During my time there, however, the management had the terrible task of completely shutting down one of the mills which was unprofitable. This was both a mammoth undertaking and an upsetting one. I saw grown men who'd worked in the factory most of their adult lives in tears, as everything they'd known evaporated. It was a sobering and difficult time.

Through the local council I became friends with Graham Bright. He was the leader of the local Conservative group and the chairman of the company that made the low-calorie sweetener, *Sweet'n Low.* Graham had a factory in Cambridgeshire and when he got elected to Parliament in 1979, he told me he needed someone and asked if I'd be willing to help run the business. It didn't happen for another few years, but in 1983 I began working for Graham and a wonderful nutter called

Dave Rains, or Rave Dains as he liked to be known! I'd love to tell you more about working with Dave, but believe me that is a book in itself!

I moved to Cambridgeshire but found that I didn't enjoy being away from home. I helped run Graham's factory for a while but it wasn't suiting me. I had been offered my old job back at Thames Board Mills, and prepared my resignation to give to Graham, but he wouldn't accept it.

"Why do you want to leave?" he asked me.

"I'm not happy living up here," I told him.

"OK, then why don't you move back to Grays and go on the road selling for us instead?" he suggested.

I agreed and spent the next several years as *Sweet'n Low* National Sales Manager. Parallel to this, I was drawn into getting involved with the beginnings of a ministry called Christian Solidarity Worldwide (CSW) and this was demanding more of my time. On more than one occasion I'd bumped into Graham at Parliament and he'd asked me,

"Why are you here? Aren't you supposed to be out somewhere selling for us?!"

I continued working for Graham until 1999 when I became full time Chief Executive of CSW. I'll tell how in the next chapter.

In retrospect, I can see how God worked to manoeuvre me into the place where He wanted me. Despite me, God moved because He had a plan.

5. CSW

David Atkinson, mentioned in the previous chapter, was a Catholic and the MP for Bournemouth East. We got to know one another through our mutual friend Graham Bright at the annual Tory conference and became good friends. David got me involved in helping him do some research for a couple of evenings each week. I say "research" – it wasn't much more than glorified filing. Through it, however, David was able to get me a pass into Westminster.

One day David chatted to me about a film he'd seen. An organisation called Christian Solidarity International (CSI), based in Switzerland, had put on an event in Westminster. Their leader, Rev Hansjürg Stückelberger, was the speaker and had shown a film about their work.

CSI was formed in Switzerland shortly after a group of people held two silent marches in protest of the imprisonment of the Russian minister Georgi Vins. Vins was a Baptist pastor who was persecuted by the Soviet authorities for his involvement in running a network of independent Baptist churches. The marches received such an amazing response that the organisers decided to set up a charity to combat religious repression and defend religious liberty.

David was impressed by what they were doing. He knew I was a Christian and asked how I felt about setting up Christian Solidarity in the UK. He told me he was due to have a meeting with CSI's leaders and suggested I accompany him.

I have to confess that at this time, I knew very little about the persecution of Christians around the world. I certainly had no inkling that this should be my "main thing" in terms of ministry. I agreed to go and meet CSI's leaders with David, but if I'm being honest, I did so reluctantly.

At the meeting it was decided that a new UK charity should be set up to establish CSI in the UK. They needed a certain number of names to do so, and I happened to be sitting in the room, so my name was put forward with the others and suddenly I was involved!

I went away not feeling particularly positive about this development, but as I drove home that evening God spoke to me quite clearly, showing me that, in fact, this was all part of His plan. He wanted me to be involved in establishing something that, to my mind, looked like a Christian version of Amnesty International. He also showed me that I would be at the heart of it. I've never really had pictures or visions, or heard God speak to me audibly, but every now and then I just *know* that God has spoken. A thought or impression comes into the mind unbidden, and carries such weight and authority that you know God has spoken. This was one of those occasions.

Diversity in the board

Thus, we established the embryonic form of what would eventually become Christian Solidarity Worldwide (CSW). CSI UK began to get going and I took a trip out to Zurich to meet representatives from the other European groups they'd set up. At that time there were small CSI bases in Switzerland, Germany, Austria, France and the Netherlands. Most of the people involved were from a non-evangelical background. One of the tasks I had was to appoint UK-based board members, and I felt quite strongly that I wanted to choose people from a more diverse spiritual heritage. With no disrespect whatsoever to my Catholic and Orthodox colleagues, I felt it might help us to reach a wider audience.

The beginnings of the board were essentially David and I, then we began to search for potential board members to join us. We also felt it wise to assemble a board of reference – essentially a group of cheerleaders for the work, who could endorse us and let others know we were an organisation worthy of support.

One of the first people who came alongside us was Rev Martin Smyth. Martin was an Ulster Unionist MP for many years and was also the

Grand Master of the Orange Order for over 20 years. This meant that we had a Catholic (David), a Pentecostal (me) and a fairly full-on Protestant (Martin), all supporting a common cause.

This made a clear statement to those who would support us in years to come. We were creating a truly ecumenical organisation that crossed boundaries. I've been aware of other charities with more conservative evangelical roots who have struggled when they've tried to widen their focus, and lost supporters as a result. But the fact that we've had characters like Gerald Coates alongside the Catholic Bishop of Brentwood on our board of reference highlighted the fact that we were interdenominational from the beginning.

The next step was to raise awareness of CSI UK's existence and begin to build a supporter base. CSI's headquarters had identified someone in the UK who they said had a large mailing list we could access, so we sought this person out and put together our first mailing. Having sent this out, however, we received response after response from people saying they weren't interested and could we remove them from our database – some of them very rudely.

Wherever this list had come from, it didn't seem appropriate to what we were doing, so we felt it was important to strengthen the board with people who had good UK church connections. I had heard of John Wildrianne through church youth camps I'd helped lead. John was the Assemblies of God World Missions Director and his wife, Doreen, was the Principal of the International Bible Training Institute (IBTI) – a Pentecostal Bible college , based in West Sussex. I had a tenuous connection to John through a mutual friend, so I thought I'd explore whether or not he might be interested in getting involved.

CSI used to produce a calendar each year, and each month featured an image of a person from a particular country. On the reverse were facts about the country and persecuted Christians in that nation. The cover page carried a message from CSI founder Hansjürg Stückelberger. We decided to produce a similar calendar for CSI UK but with a message from David Atkinson on the cover page. I felt the fact that a Christian MP was involved in this venture would interest people. A friend gave a copy of the calendar to John Wildrianne and in due course he agreed to meet me.

John was an amazing, larger than life character, and liked nothing better than a late night chat over a glass of quality whiskey. We became very good friends and years later he conducted our wedding ceremony when Wendy and I married. John was instrumental in moving the organisation forward, partly through his role as AoG missions director, and partly through organising special weekends at the IBTI with a focus on the persecuted Church. John travelled constantly and promoted the charity wherever he could.

John introduced me to Brian Edwards, who was the Elim Pentecostal movement's missions director. Brian also agreed to join the board and, like John, had travelled extensively, which meant that he was very knowledgeable and a great support during the early years. Other early board members included Gilbert Kirby, who served as the General Secretary of the Evangelical Alliance and was also Principal of the London Bible College, and Bernard Porter, a pastor who led an AoG church in Paddington, north London.

It's always good to have a lawyer as part of a board if possible, and that position was filled by Ernest Leland, a solicitor from Romford. I phoned him up one Saturday morning and asked if he'd be willing to get involved. Ernie turned out to be an incredible force for good on the board – a real man of God and prayer warrior. He remained on the board until only a few years ago and died in 2017. In the late 1980s Ernie travelled to Romania on our behalf, to visit a Christian lawyer who was in trouble with the government, and a London based barrister, Franklin Evans, accompanied him. Franklin came to visit and tell me about the trip later and we ended up becoming very close friends. He joined our board too and was also best man at my wedding.

When I became Chief Executive in 1999 and stepped down from the board, Franklin took over as chair for the next 12 years. He still remains a board member to this day, and has been a very faithful friend and ministry partner. I could tell you a host of stories about Franklin over the years, but as he's a barrister and a judge, I might find myself on the wrong side of the law!

We have been very fortunate that during the past 40 years, we have only had four chairmen. After Franklin we had the wonderfully wise and pastoral Bishop John Perry and, at present, we are blessed to be guided by former diplomat David Taylor.

More connections

In the mid-80s I was invited to speak to the Parliamentary Wives Christian Fellowship, which at the time was run by Susie Sainsbury and Betty Mawhinney. Of all places we met in the Speaker's Bedroom (not really where he slept, but more of a museum piece). Afterwards, a lady called Janet Dunn expressed an interest in helping us, and later served on our Board. Janet's husband, Bob, was MP for Dartford and later held the post of schools minister.

It was Bob who suggested I talk to another person on the education team, who turned out to be Baroness Caroline Cox. He thought she would be a great person to strengthen our board. I met with Caroline in the House of Lords. She asked me point blank,

"What can I do for you?"

The only thing I could think of was,

"Join our board!" and she agreed.

Our early board meetings were held in London at Norman Shaw North – an amazing Grade I listed building, formerly known as New Scotland Yard, the administrative HQ of the Metropolitan Police Commissioner. After Caroline had been on the board for a couple of years, we decided to have a small conference to promote the work.

We found an appropriate space in the Westminster area and Father George Calciu from Romania was one of the speakers, along with Baroness Cox.

As an aside, I remember being interviewed that day by a young reporter from Essex Radio. His name was Peter Kerridge, and he went on to become the very successful CEO of Premier Christian Radio, which has carried CSW's programme *Voice for the Voiceless* since the very first week they went on air in June 1995.

Our relationship with Premier has been very special, and they always embraced both Stuart and I as members of the Premier family. Almost every presenter that ever worked for Premier has presented our show, from Cindy Kent to Martin Mitchell, Dave Rose, Helen Featherstone Phil Mercer, John Pantry, Maria Rodrigues, Charmaine Noble-McClean… the list could go on. For a number of years now we have been blessed to have Premier's longest serving presenter, Rick Easter, fronting the programme. Rick really believes in what we do at CSW and is a special friend to us. Of course, he also makes producing the programme a lot of fun!

Over the years, Caroline Cox became more and more immersed in the work of CSI UK and I recall her saying to me one day in Oxford, as we walked to get some lunch,

"You know, I really feel the Lord is calling me to make this my main interest."

Until then she had held a mainly figurehead position in CSI UK and was a great ambassador for the work, but she wanted to play a more active role in what we were doing.

Becoming independent

Inevitably, organisations grow and adapt, and some need to change in order to respond to the challenges of their context. Over time, collectively, the board of CSI UK made a case for us functioning as an independent charity, separate from the CSI parent organisation. Initially, I wanted to try and make things work as they were. Especially in the beginning, CSI gave us a great deal of support and though they didn't provide complete financial support, they helped to shore up the charity when needed. I didn't want to break away from them unnecessarily, but I recognised that the board had solid reasons for wanting to do so.

The parting of the ways came when the Swiss HQ wanted us to lodge a copy of our UK supporter database in Zurich, if we were to remain a part of the organisation. Of course we couldn't legally do this, and the board weren't happy to in any case. By this time we had worked hard to build a great base of supporters who were investing in projects we had initiated ourselves. This was when the decision was made to become an independent charity, made official in 1997, after which we became known as Christian Solidarity Worldwide (CSW). We had looked at various possibilities for a completely new name, but realised that the Christian Solidarity brand was really beginning to get recognition in the UK. One week I was praying with my friend and prayer partner, Paul Heffer (more of him later), and he really felt the Lord telling him we should simply replace "International" with "Worldwide". So quite simply we obeyed!

Since the early 80s I had been travelling constantly, speaking at churches all over the country – mainly to Pentecostal churches to begin with, because those were my natural connections. At the height of my busyness I would get up at the crack of dawn on a Sunday morning and drive all the way from Grays to Manchester or Liverpool, speak at a church service, then drive all the way back to speak at another service in the south in the evening. Much of the support network was built by sheer hard graft and having a consistent presence in key churches.

On one typically long day I found myself speaking at a meeting in north London. I had been on the road all day and arrived at the church for the evening service. The pastor and his wife were an older couple who lived on the church premises. I arrived at 6.00pm for their 6.30pm meeting and they invited me into their small kitchen.

"Would you like a cup of tea?" the pastor's wife asked.

I'd already stopped for refreshments on the road, so I declined, but said it in a joking manner.

"I'd better not, thank you, otherwise I'll probably want to go to the loo halfway through the service!"

The service began and it transpired that the pastor's wife was the church organist. After we'd sung the first hymn, she stopped playing and said in a loud stage whisper to her husband, in the pulpit,

"Why don't you get a glass of water for the speaker?"

The pastor responded in an even louder stage whisper.

"With his problem, that's the last thing he needs!"

I managed to get through the service, but couldn't help but wonder what the rest of the congregation were thinking.

"That poor man. I wonder what's wrong with him?!"

There is a nice postscript to the story, however. More than twenty years later I was speaking at a church in High Wycombe and an elderly gentleman came up for a chat. It turned out that he had been the pastor of the aforementioned church. He told me, "After your visit we regularly supported CSW and the church has done ever since." He wasn't sure if I'd remember him. I assured him I did, but didn't let on the reason why!

At the time of writing, we have been going through a rebranding process for the charity that will reposition us for the future. In today's global/political context, our full name can lead to misconceptions and assumptions about our aims and agenda, that in no way reflect the reality of what we do, and which in some circumstances are unhelpful to our work. We are already known and highly regarded as CSW in many circles, so it was a very natural step to move to the use of the acronym, with the addition of the strapline, "Everyone. Free to believe." More on that in a later chapter.

6. Key People

Today CSW has specialist teams of advocates working in more than 25 nations across Asia, Africa, the Middle East and Latin America, who defend the right to freedom of religion or belief, but every organisation has to begin somewhere. This chapter pays tribute to some of those people who were there at the beginning, and who were instrumental in CSW's growth and development.

Initially, we had no paid employees. We had a board, but no one on the ground to do the work, so like most fledgling organisations, members of the board got involved with operational matters, simply because there was no one else to do it.

The first person to be paid on a part-time basis was a PR person, loaned to us by David Atkinson, who was actually his executive assistant. David Bick's initial task was to handle the responses we received from our early mailings, seeking supporters. However, CSI's Swiss office funded the post, because we had literally no money. He helped to produce a leaflet called "Time for Action Now" which highlighted the persecution of Christians in Eastern Europe. At that time, what was happening in Europe was our major focus, simply because that was the extent of our knowledge. We started political lobbying in order to raise awareness and began to gain political advocates who might be able to exert pressure to help certain individuals and bring about change.

Early administrative support came from Stan White, an Assemblies of God pastor from Gravesend in Kent. Stan worked part-time for an organisation called Christian Mission to the Communist World, formed by Richard Wurmbrand, the Romanian minister who was imprisoned for a total of fourteen years by the communist regime. The organisation would eventually become Release International, as it is known today. Stan agreed to process donations for us and I opened a bank account for CSW with NatWest in Romford, which we still have to this day. The fact that we were working with an organisation run by Richard Wurmbrand was kept quiet, because at the time the Pentecostal movement wasn't comfortable with the idea of people smuggling Bibles into countries illegally.

Our first full time post of National Director came in the form of a five-foot Scotsman who wasn't really Scottish, with the unforgettable name, Ronald McDonald! Ron had been brought up in Scotland, spoke with a Scottish accent, and occasionally wore a kilt, but wasn't born there. He was a former communist who had been radically converted, and now lived in Colchester.

Because Ron loved Scotland so much, we gave him the task of raising support in the north. He travelled around the Scottish churches, speaking about the work and raising awareness. He did a great job and to this day there is still a strong Scottish supporter base for CSW. Ron worked with us from 1981–85.

Roger Shelley was someone I'd worked with at Thames Board Mills. He was a timekeeper there, clocking workers in an out. I knew he was a Christian and I invited him to join our board. After he had served on the board for a while, he was made redundant from the Mill, and the timing worked out for us to appoint him as our second National Director.

Roger worked from his home in Leigh-on-Sea and this became our main office address for a while. So, essentially, we worked out of Roger's spare bedroom! Later he found a local church who were willing to partition off a small room and allowed us to use that as our office. It had an external door, so we could go in and out without disrupting the church. We had an official opening for this small office. David Atkinson came down from London and Father George Calciu attended too.

As the ministry grew, it became a challenge for Roger to keep pace and it was clear he needed some help, so we engaged our second employee as an office assistant. After a few years Roger moved on, and his moving coincided with me receiving a letter from a young man in his early 20s called Simon George, who'd seen our literature and was asking if we had any vacancies.

In time, Simon who came from Wolverhampton took on the post of National Director and he came with a much bigger vision than simply raising funds for the organisation. Simon helped us to begin campaigning more effectively in Parliament. One of the first Parliamentary campaigns we ran was for some Christian Princesses in Ethiopia. He also took the initiative to train himself in fundraising and launched several advocacy initiatives.

For some years we had a supporter magazine called Response, and through this magazine we told the stories of many people who were being persecuted and explained how and where people could write to lobby the relevant authorities. Sometimes we would include a postcard, so that all people had to do was sign and post it. We have always encouraged a practical approach to advocacy, coupled with prayer. Simon stayed with CSW for around four years before setting up his own fundraising consultancy. We've remained friends ever since and a few years ago Simon re-joined CSW as one of our Trustees. I was once his boss but now he's mine!

Frank Collins worked for CSW for a year. Frank was a good friend and prayer partner of mine. He had been in the SAS and was the first soldier to storm the building via the roof during the famous Iranian Embassy siege that took place in London from April 30 to May 5 in 1980.

Frank came to know Christ through the witness of an American special forces colleague. After he left "the regiment" he got ordained as a Church of England minister, and became Chaplain to the SAS Territorials. Like many former service personnel who have worked in dangerous circumstances, however, he found it difficult to adjust to civilian or church life.

Nevertheless, Frank had a tremendous love for the Lord and a passion to win people to Christ. He loved telling his story and he was the type of person who could fill churches. People flocked to see and hear from a real-life SAS hero, and his book *Baptism of Fire*, was a great success. I believe Frank was the fulfilment of a prophetic picture I once had.

At one point we lived in Burwell, Cambridgeshire, and attended a Baptist church that was struggling a little at the time. It was an old-fashioned building that had large windows with deep sills down each side of the hall, and a balcony overlooking it. The congregation at Burwell were rattling around in this building, but one day I had a clear picture from God where I saw the place packed with people. The floor and the balcony were full, and people were even sitting on the window sills.

I invited Frank to come and speak at the church one Saturday night. He came to give his testimony and that night was exactly as I'd seen it in my picture – absolutely packed, such that people desperate for a seat had to sit on the window sills.

Frank was married with four kids and when he left the regiment, his wife Claire had hoped they could settle down to a more normal life. As a member of the SAS he had travelled constantly and each time he left home, he could never let Claire know where he was going. Sadly, Frank struggled to readjust. He would still spend long periods away from home, even while he was working for CSW, and would frequently sleep in a VW camper van that he had, parked outside our offices. Consequently, it put a great strain on his marriage.

The last time I spoke to Frank was on his mobile phone as he was going around a supermarket. He'd turned his phone off for a couple of days and had just turned it back on when I called. He told me he had almost 50 voicemail messages – all people wanting him to go and speak at churches. He didn't like to turn anyone down, even though it was really too much for him. I remember telling him that he ought to get an agent, so that someone else could say no for him.

Frank had been due to speak at a church on behalf of CSW that weekend, but he told me,

"I just can't do it, Merv."

"Why?" I asked.

"I've had this headache on and off for three months," he explained.

I told him he should go and see his doctor, but he wouldn't do that.

"Regiment men don't get headaches," he said.

Two days later I received a phone call from the Daily Mail newspaper telling me that Frank had been found dead in the garage of his literary agent's house, having taken his own life. I was so sad to see this brave man who had survived many brutal situations unable to cope with life outside the regiment.

* * *

In 1993, we appointed a new National Director – a person who would prove to be a key figure in the organisation for years to come. The connection was made by Terry Hanford, an AoG pastor who was on our board. Terry was also on the broadcasting council of the AoG, and one of his fellow council members was a man called Stuart Windsor. Stuart was the assistant pastor at a Pentecostal church in Widnes and also ran his own media company called Spirit Free Communications. When we needed a new national director, Terry told me,

"There's this guy who might fit the bill, Stuart Windsor. You've met him."

I couldn't really recall ever having met Stuart, but I told Terry,

"OK, if he's interested, tell him to write to me with his CV."

Apparently, I had spoken at Stuart's church several years earlier and he had filmed the service. I vaguely remembered chatting to a white haired guy at the end of the service who said he'd send me a copy of the video. That was Stuart.

A couple of weeks later I was sitting at home one evening and the phone rang.

"Hello Merv, it's Stu here," the voice said cheerily. I didn't know anyone of that name, so I said,

"Oh, Stu who?"

"You know, Stu," he responded.

"I'm sorry, I don't know who you are," I said.

"Stu from Widnes," he offered.

"I still can't place you," I told him.

"Terry Hanford told me to call you about this job that's going," he eventually explained and the penny finally dropped.

"Ah, OK, Stuart. Well, write to me and send me your CV and we'll go from there."

"Send you what?"

"Your CV, your employment history."

"CV… Oh, OK."

Well, Stuart didn't have a CV, but a couple of days later he faxed one through to me, entirely hand-written. He had an interesting background and relevant experience, so I ended up giving him the job.

Stu was a larger than life character and when he began working for us,

I was still in the role of Chairman. He would call me every single day, and always at 6.15pm precisely. Unfortunately, this was dinner time in our house. After several mealtimes had been interrupted I said to him,

"Stu, could you call me either earlier or later, but not at 6.15pm because that's when we're in the middle of our dinner."

"Oh yes, of course!" he replied. But he carried on calling me at 6.15pm no matter what I said!

Between 1993–99 Stuart and Caroline Cox were responsible for the huge growth in CSW's supporter base. Caroline was very well known and churches loved having a Baroness come and speak to them, so she was a great ambassador for the work. Stuart had an incredible work ethic and threw his heart and soul into the ministry – much as I had done to help launch CSW. Stuart would drive the length and breadth of the country to represent us at churches and he never turned down an invitation – meaning that on more than one occasion he was double or even treble booked!

Caring for the persecuted church was Stuart's life calling and great passion, one which would take him all over the world, finding himself on the receiving end of God's grace and miraculous intervention time and time again. Stuart sadly, and suddenly passed away in 2017. He was a complete one-off and my closest friend and partner. I miss him loads. At his memorial service, attended by hundreds, I spoke about our shared passion for Arsenal FC. I told how we would both, in our separate homes, sit down and watch the football on Sky, and we would text each other throughout the game. The problem was Stu was always very formal in his messages and so it would go something like this:

Dear Merv,

Glad Sanchez is playing

God bless

Stu

Dear Merv

How did Giroud miss that?

God bless

Stu

Dear Merv

YESSS

God bless

Stu.

It is well worth reading his full story in the book *God's Adventurer* (Monarch, 2011).

A change of focus

During the years 1993–1999, CSW became involved in a number of practical aid projects around the world, which ran parallel to our main work of advocacy for those suffering persecution for their faith.

While Baroness Cox and Stuart were both working for the organisation, there was a humanitarian crisis in Nagorno-Karabakh, as the area tried to recover from the Armenian-Azerbaijan war that had lasted for six years. CSW were involved in sending plane-loads of aid to the area. Stuart was made an honorary citizen of the territory as a result.

For many years we also ran a Christian School in Hetauda, Nepal. This was a project we took over from CSI in Zurich.

We also sent aid to war-torn Sudan, and one of Caroline's most successful projects was to virtually singlehandedly introduce foster care into Russia. We still campaigned for religious freedom, and had dedicated staff to do so, but many of the practical projects ate up staff and resources.

It became apparent to me that people responded more to a humanitarian crisis than they did to the plight of individuals in need of advocacy. This is entirely understandable, as feeding the hungry, drilling wells and delivering medicine are all highly visible activities, but these activities were beginning to dilute the reason that CSW existed.

As a board, we began a conversation that would eventually lead to me becoming Chief Executive and CSW getting back to its roots, but I needed some convincing to give up my job and commit to the work full time.

John Wildrianne asked me several times to assume the role of Chief Executive, but I was reticent to put any stress on the organisation's finances. However, a growing burden for those around the world who were being persecuted and in need of support convinced me it was now the right thing to do.

On one occasion a Romanian girl who'd emigrated to the UK came to speak at an event we held in Parliament. She was campaigning on behalf of her brother, who had been imprisoned for his faith. She told her story, which was powerful and moving.

"I grew up next door to one of the prison camps. Every night, as a young girl, I lay in bed listening to people inside the camp screaming. I knew that there were people from my church in that camp. I knew that many other Christians were being held there, too, and terribly mistreated.

Because of this, I made up my mind that I would never give my life to Christ, because I was so fearful of what would happen to me if I did.

But one night at church, the preacher spoke from the verse 1 John 4:18: '*There is no fear in love, but perfect love drives out fear...*' That night I accepted Jesus into my heart and his love came and cast out the fear I felt."

When she was older she moved to the West, but her brother was put in prison, so she began campaigning for his release. He was eventually set free and also emigrated to the West to be with his sister. But one day God spoke to her and said, "Why have you stopped campaigning? What about your brother who is still in prison?"

She was puzzled by this.

"I haven't got any other brothers," she told the Lord.

"What about the people you heard screaming when you were younger? Are they not your family?"

She told us,

"It was then that I realised that any follower of Christ is as much my family as my blood brother. When Christians are being persecuted for their faith, that is happening to my family."

This really hit me.

If my brother or sister, son or daughter were in prison because of their faith, I'd be shouting it from the rooftops. I decided then that I wouldn't let a minute go by without talking about my brothers and sisters in Christ who are suffering for their faith, because they are family.

So it was that in 1999 I became CSW's Chief Executive, finally giving up my job at *Sweet'n Low*. The decision was made at a Board weekend down at the IBTI, and was sealed when the board members gathered round and laid hands on me. Leading the prayers was Bishop Richard Hare. As soon as he touched me I went down under the power of the Spirit – the only time that has ever happened to me. It was a wonderful experience and seemed to me to be the Holy Spirit's seal on my appointment.

Bishop Richard Hare was a very special man who joined our board in 1992 as he retired from 21 years as Bishop of Pontefract. Richard was the first Episcopal participant in the Charismatic Renewal which swept the country in the 1970s and he was quite a character.

I will never forget the first time we met. It was in 1992 in a restaurant just around the corner from Church House, Westminster. Several of us had adjourned there for lunch during CSW's annual conference, and I found myself sitting opposite this man who I had heard so much about. As he was a Bishop, I thought he would be the ideal person to say grace before the meal, but I wasn't ready for what happened next. In a packed London restaurant, he made us all stand up and then sung at the top of his voice, "Be present at our table Lord!"

That was the beginning of a long friendship which was a special blessing to me personally and to CSW and its supporters. Who could ever forget the unique "Pentecostal" blessings he gave every year at the end of our London conferences, always ending with a loud cry of "Hallelujah!"

In his later years, I used to look forward to my annual visit to speak at the CSW Cumbria Action Group, because it meant I got to stay the night with Richard in his tiny, damp little cottage in Mirehouse near Keswick. Before retiring to bed, a highlight for me was sipping a brandy while turning over a deck of playing cards Richard had memorised. He had a near photographic memory and used to do this every night before he went to bed, because he was terrified of getting dementia. Incidentally, when he shuffled the pack, he only had to turn each card over once to memorise the order.

When I became Chief Executive CSW was struggling with its finances for a number of reasons and, with the support of the board, I needed to make some difficult decisions. One was to get back to the heart of what CSW is all about, as illustrated in the story above – advocacy on behalf of those who are being persecuted.

So the decision was made to stop our practical aid programmes, but without leaving people who were relying on us high and dry. We made plans to transition those projects to other organisations. Soon after this, Caroline Cox amicably decided to set up her own charity called HART to take on many of the projects she herself had pioneered.

With a reorganised structure, CSW began to focus again on advocacy. I had spent much of my time up to this point lobbying in Parliament, so we had lots of friends in Westminster and many high-level contacts. I was also determined that going forward CSW would be known for the quality and reliability of its information, so that to others we could be a central hub for them to learn what was happening to people of faith all around the world. That decision was to become the turning point and the beginning of the CSW you see today.

7. Romania

It was the beginning of 1985 when I first travelled to Romania and experienced first-hand how difficult life could be for the believers living there. The trip had been organised by CSI's head office in Zurich, and the plan was for me and my travelling companion to rendezvous with three American congressmen: Frank Wolf, Tony Hall and Chris Smith.

This is the trip, mentioned in the preface of this book, on which I was accompanied by the footballer Justin Fashanu. Justin was at the height of his fame. A classic goal he'd scored for Norwich City against Liverpool was constantly shown during the title sequence of Match of the Day and at the time of our trip he had just been transferred to Nottingham Forest for $1 Million. He was the first black player to achieve such heights.

I had limited information about the trip. Other than knowing I was to travel with Justin, then connect with the congressmen in Romania, along with some of our Swiss colleagues, I didn't know too much about the purpose of the visit. The agenda was being handled by our Swiss HQ.

Justin and I met at Heathrow airport and hit it off immediately. He was a great guy. He attended the Christian Centre in Nottingham and had been led to the Lord by a car dealer by the name of Terry Carpenter, who coincidentally many years later became the father-in-law of my nephew James. The previous night Justin had shared his testimony at a Billy Graham rally in Sheffield and it was big news that a top football star had given his life to the Lord. By the time the plane landed in Romania, we were bosom buddies.

Justin and I, our Swiss colleagues, and the US congressmen were all supposed to converge on Bucharest on the same day. For some reason this plan had gone awry and we arrived there a couple of days before everyone else. It looked like an unfortunate mistake, but in retrospect I can see it was entirely God's doing.

We stepped off the plane and made our way out of the airport. Neither of us had ever been to a place quite like this before. Both of us felt a tangible sense of oppression. It was quite literally in the air; a spiritual heaviness. There was no one there to meet us and, a few phone calls later, we realised that we were on our own, for now at least. Hailing a taxi, we made our way to our designated hotel.

The 1980s was one of the worst decades in Romanian history. The leader of the Communist regime, Nicolae Ceausescu, had enforced an austerity policy on the nation. Part of the ill-advised plan was to pay back all the debt the nation owed, often ahead of time, so that Romania could become a completely independent, self-sustaining country. What nation has ever achieved that?

The result was a bleak time that impacted the everyday lives of Romanian people, such that there were constant food shortages and ongoing disruption to basic services such as electricity and water supply. It became commonplace to queue for hours on end outside grocery stores to buy overpriced loaves of bread as the economy imploded. The government began to ration staple foods and Ceausescu issued his "Rational Eating Programme" – an attempt to reduce the daily calorie intake for every person by around 15%, as he claimed, "Romanians are eating too much!" A year later he tried to reduce it further. Food was so scarce that even the chickens one could buy weighed less than half a pound and were smaller than pigeons.

A drive through grey, foreboding streets reflected the national mood as Justin and I arrived at our hotel. We decided that the first thing we should do was pray. We dropped our bags by the door of our shared room and proceeded to have one of the most powerful, impactful times of prayer I've ever had with just one other person. Afterwards, I felt it would be a good idea to let the British Embassy know that we were in Bucharest, especially considering Justin's high public profile.

The hotel concierge gave us directions to the embassy and we walked there. The Chargé d'affaires was flustered by our appearance and clearly not pleased to see us. It spoke volumes about the dictatorship regime Romania lived under, that he motioned to us not to speak until we had been escorted down into the basement of the embassy. It was effectively an insulated bunker – the only room in the whole building they were certain was not bugged. The door closed behind us and the Chargé d'affaires spoke.

"This is the only place where it's safe for us to talk," he began. "Have a seat."

Justin and I sat opposite him across a small table.

"You can't stay," he said, bluntly. "You'll have to get on the next flight home."

"Why?" I queried.

"It's not safe for you," the Ambassador replied. "There is security everywhere. One false move and the authorities will come down on you like a ton of bricks."

"We're not going home," I insisted. "We're here now and we've got to meet with our colleagues in a couple of days."

"Why are you here early?" he wanted to know.

"I don't know," I told him. "There was some mix-up with the dates."

The Chargé d'affaires knew about the visit of the US congressman, but he still wasn't happy. Eventually he advised us,

"Look, go back to your hotel and stay there. Keep your heads down and don't go out, and especially don't talk to anyone."

We returned to the hotel and had another long time of prayer, bringing the situation before God. As we were praying, Father George Calciu came to my mind. Fr. Calciu was an Orthodox priest who was critical of Ceauşescu's repression of the Romanian people and therefore considered by the government to be an enemy of the State. He had been imprisoned for a total of twenty-one years.

We had been campaigning for Fr. Calciu for some time. The MP David Alton had recently visited Romania and, at David Atkinson's request, had enquired after Fr. Calciu's wellbeing. He'd been told by the authorities that Fr. Calciu had been released from prison and was fine. We, however, suspected that he was still under house arrest. He may have been released from prison, but was he really free? It was almost impossible to find out the truth without seeing it for ourselves.

As Justin and I prayed I felt strongly that we had arrived in Bucharest early for a reason – and that reason was to seek out Fr. Calciu and discover the truth about his treatment by the authorities.

"I think God is telling us to go and find Father George Calciu," I told Justin.

"Who is he?" he asked.

I gave him the background to the story. Fash was essentially up for anything, so he said,

"Right, well let's go and find him then."

There was just one problem.

"I don't know his address," I said, "or where to start looking for him."

"Did you notice we passed a small church on the walk back from the Embassy," Fash said. "I think it was an Anglican church. Let's go back there and ask. Someone there must know where Fr. Calciu lives."

* * *

I won't repeat what happened on that attempted visit. Suffice to say that although we didn't get to see him personally, Fr. Calciu learned of our visit, and this greatly encouraged him.

After our unwelcome brush with the *Securitate* outside Fr. Calciu's apartment block, we returned to our hotel. The concierge tried very hard to allocate us a different, "better" hotel room and I resisted. After being repeatedly told about the security risks in Romania, and how the authorities monitored every conversation, I suspected the only reason the hotel wanted to move us was because the new room had been specially bugged and they could listen to our conversations.

"But sir," the concierge said. "The air conditioning is much better!"

"No, we're fine, thank you," I insisted. "Our room is very nice."

Fash was puzzled but went along with me and I explained my suspicions. They were later confirmed by the fact that, from that moment, and for the rest of our trip, we were followed around by at least a dozen not-very-discrete secret police – the Securitate. It was very James Bond-esque. Men in trench coats and hats peered around corners. The same faces appeared nearby us again and again. Maybe the lack of discretion was deliberate? A message to say, "We're watching you."

Shortly after we'd arrived back in our hotel room we received a phone call to say that our presence was demanded back at the British Embassy and we were to go there immediately. As we walked back, Fash incorrigibly waved at the people assigned to follow us, even though I urged him not to. He even called out, "Nice to see you! How are you, alright?"

If possible, the Chargé d'affaires was colder with us than he'd been before.

"You'll be sent home," he said flatly. "I told you to keep your heads down and you didn't listen. Worse still, you were arrested by the *Securitate*. Why did you do it?"

"Because that's what we came here to do," I told him.

"Well, you're going to be sent back," he informed us.

He then told us that he had no idea how we had even managed to get into the country, because our Swiss colleagues had been refused entry. Right before the trip their visas had been revoked and they'd been instructed not to travel. For some mysterious reason we had been allowed in.

"The authorities were going to allow you to stay, but since you've already got into trouble, you'll be sent home tomorrow," the Chargé d'affaires informed us.

In the event, we weren't sent home. The Romanian government needed the visit of the US congressman and one of their party, Frank Wolf, discovered that we were about to be sent home. He insisted that if we were deported, the congressman would cancel their trip. The Romanian authorities weren't about to let that happen, because Congress was due to vote on the issue of whether to grant Romania "most favoured nation" (MFN) status. Having MFN status would give Romania significant international trade benefits to prop up its languishing economy, such as low tariffs and increased trade.

The Romanian authorities also had to try to prove to the US congressmen that religious freedom existed in Romania, so they were caught in a Catch 22. Now that Frank Wolf had heard about what was happening to us, they couldn't possibly deport us.

One experience I had in Romania showed me just how paranoid the government really was, and just how intense the security was. I had noticed that our hotel lift had no button for floor 11. The numbers skipped from 10 to 12. Being inquisitive, I couldn't help but wonder, "What's on floor 11?" One day I decided to find out, so I went to explore on my own.

I got in the elevator and got out at floor 10, then took the stairs up one flight to floor 11. I opened the door onto a long corridor and crept along until I came to a door. Gingerly, I opened the door and glanced inside. It was a huge room, filled with row upon row of girls wearing headphones, all busy scribbling down information on pads. No one looked up and no one saw me. It wasn't until that moment that I truly appreciated what I'd been told by many people:

"Everything is recorded. Every conversation is listened to."

Once Frank Wolf and his colleagues had arrived in Bucharest, Fash and I accompanied them on several official visits. It was then that I began to meet some amazing Christian people who were suffering persecution under the communist regime.

We travelled to visit many different places, ferried around in minibuses. We visited a number of churches and were usually asked to say a few words or preach a short sermon. Around that time the chorus *Be Bold, Be Strong* was new and very popular. Fash and I taught it to Congressman Chris Smith's assistant, Mary, and in many of the churches we visited, the three of us sung it to the congregation.

We were late for virtually every appointment we had, because at the end of each church service people mobbed us. Numerous pieces of paper were slipped into our hands. They contained information about people's repressed situations, snippets of their stories, or simply heartrending messages saying, "Help us get out of here." Knowing that the State was listening, it was a desperate attempt to get information to the "outside world".

I remember one particular trip. We were at least three hours late for a visit to a church in the countryside. It was the middle of June and very hot and humid. We thought that in the end it might be a wasted trip. We were, after all, three hours late, so assumed they would have had their service and gone home.

When we arrived, we could hear the congregation singing. The church had a corrugated iron structure, so we knew it must be boiling hot inside. The people were overjoyed to see us and I was struck by the sheer joy they had.

After the church service ended we were invited to eat all together. I'm the world's fussiest eater; so much so that to this day I'm wary of visiting other people's houses for dinner because I don't know what I'll get. But these poor people had laid on the best banquet they could for us. They'd saved up for months in order to put on Romanian delicacies. This included things like bean paste with a small amount of smoked meat, *Ciorba de Burta* (beef tripe soup), and fish soup with the bones left in.

I really appreciated the huge sacrifice these people had made to give us the best they possibly could, but all I wanted to do was throw up! They had no fridges, so bottles of drink were buried in the ground in an effort to keep them cool. I drank as much as possible and avoided the food!

After this visit we were scheduled to travel to Oradea, a city in north-western Romania. It was home, even in those communist rule days, to the largest Baptist church in Europe. It actually had a ridiculously small building for the size of its congregation (around 3,000 members), purely because they couldn't get permission for anything larger.

We flew to Oradea and were collected from the airport by various cars. Fash and I shared one car. The young man driving us spoke English so we tried chatting to him, but he refused to speak and kept pointing to his dashboard. He was letting us know that his car was bugged and we couldn't speak freely.

One of the pastors of the church was Rev Paul Negrut. He was an amazing guy and absolutely fearless and uncompromising in his preaching, which made him an enemy of the government. As our party arrived at the church a wedding was in full flow. It took us almost 10 minutes to work our way from the entrance of the church to the platform – the place was jam packed with people. People stood in the aisles, perched on the window sills, and stood outside listening. I felt a bit like a gate crasher, arriving in the midst of someone's wedding!

We had been followed to the church by a vast number of *Securitate*. The scale of the oppression was astonishing. Later Paul Negrut told me that even he'd never seen anything like it. My heart sank as I learned that in the evening, after the service, we were invited to another banquet. It was organised by the local government.

Paul Negrut later told me, "Before your visit we were treated like criminals, but that evening we were like honoured guests". On the menu that night was sheep's brains and as soon as I learned what it was, I felt queasy, opting to drink lots of water and eat as little as possible. I feigned illness and told my guests I had a bad stomach!

I remember shaking hands with one government minister and saying to him,

"Thank you for inviting us."

He looked at me coldly and responded in a stilted accent,

"I didn't invite you. I would never do that. I was made to invite you. You'll never come back to Romania again."

That was the end of my first trip to this nation. A journey of bleak contrasts – the awful oppressive atmosphere with its uncompromising communist regime, and the simplicity of life and deep, genuine joy of the Christians who lived under it.

8. Father Calciu

When I first met Father George Calciu in person it was in the middle of a church meeting and although I knew who he was, he didn't have a clue who I was. He was travelling throughout the UK and was in Burgess Hill, speaking at the Assemblies of God church there. For some reason I was running late and the meeting had begun with some worship. It was my job to introduce him, because I had visited his native Romania.

I hurried to the platform and saw Fr. Calciu sitting there. His face was very serious looking – so much so that one might think he was in a terrible mood. I acknowledged him briefly and then I had to introduce him. I spoke about my first trip to Romania and told the story of how I had tracked down his apartment and tried to visit him. At that point I looked around and an amazing smile had spread across his face. He simply radiated God's love and I thought, "If anyone's face has ever reflected Jesus, it's this man's." As I went to sit down, he got up and hugged me tightly. That was the beginning of a really strong friendship; he would call me his spiritual son.

After his eventual release from prison, then house arrest, he had been allowed to emigrate to the US. The MP David Alton had been instrumental in getting him released. He had settled in the Washington area, and had subsequently been invited to the UK to tour the country and speak at a number of churches – hence his visit to Burgess Hill.

At this point, I must make special mention of David Alton (now Lord Alton). Throughout the forty years I have been engaged in this work, he has been a constant and courageous voice for religious freedom, and also for many other Christian issues. I pay tribute to this modern day Wilberforce. He has been a wonderful ally in so many causes.

I hadn't known a huge amount about Fr. Calciu's life until then – other than the bare facts of his imprisonment for his faith. The Romanian authorities had marked him as an enemy of the State and he had been falsely imprisoned for 21 years overall, across two terms. It wasn't until we met face to face and became friends that I learned more about his amazing life.

* * *

When Ceaușescu came to power, Fr. Calciu was caught up in a wide ranging "purge" of Christian leaders initiated by the dictator. He was accused of being part of the "Iron Guard". This was a far-right political movement that was ultra-nationalistic, strongly anti-communist, and promoted Eastern Orthodox Christianity. Of course, Fr. Calciu was never a part of that movement, but that didn't matter to the authorities and, after a show trial he was sentenced to 15 years in prison. At one point he was in prison with Richard Wurmbrand, author of the bestselling book *Tortured for Christ* and founder of Voice of the Martyrs organisation.

At this point in his life he wasn't yet a priest. The conditions in the prison were absolutely appalling and he nearly died. Around him were many Christians, some of whom died in prison, and this had a profound effect on him. It was then that he felt God calling him to the priesthood. When he was eventually released from prison he was ordained and given a parish to pastor. At the same time he worked as Professor of French at the Orthodox seminary in Bucharest.

Fr. Calciu had a big heart for young people. During Lent in 1979 he set about preaching a 6-week series of sermons. They were very popular and attracted a lot of young people, so the church began to be packed out every week. After the fourth week, however, he arrived early at his church to prepare for the meeting and found it closed up with the locks changed. Since he couldn't get into his own church, when the crowd gathered in due course, he just preached in the churchyard.

The following week when he arrived at his church, he found the gates to the churchyard had been chained shut, so he preached to the crowd on the street. He had concluded his 6-week series, but then the authorities had him arrested.

It was at this point that Fr. Calciu came onto CSW's radar. We heard this man, a high profile Christian, had been put in prison and we began to gather prayer support for him and campaign for his release. This was significant in the development of CSW's ministry. We had strong roots in the Pentecostal movement and supporting an Orthodox priest would have put some supporters outside of their comfort zones. Certainly, there was a huge difference in theology. But we had a quote from Fr. Calciu that greatly motivated us to action:

"Why do good men remain silent? We need you to speak up for us when we are no longer able to speak for ourselves."

These words sum up the mission that CSW has pursued for the last 40 years.

It was during Fr. Calciu's second prison term that the authorities tried to rid themselves of him forever.

He spent the first 15 months in complete solitary confinement. He had no human contact with anyone, apart from the silent guard who delivered the bare minimum of sustenance – some water every day, and a small amount of bread every other day. When his wife was eventually allowed to visit him, he hadn't spoken in over a year, and he really struggled to form words.

It was frightening to think that a person might forget how to speak through lack of use, so after that visit Fr. Calciu began speaking to the cockroaches in his cell. Once a week he would also go through the Orthodox liturgy as if he was conducting a service.

Eventually, he was moved into a cell with two other men. Initially, he was thrilled about this because at last he would have some companionship – but he didn't know who these men were. It turned out that one was a serial killer, and the other had murdered his own mother. He had been intentionally placed with these men, who had been given instructions to murder the priest in a fight, making it look like an accident. Fr. Calciu was so well known in the West that the authorities dare not assassinate him outright, so instead they sought to contrive his death.

He was unaware of this to begin with, but then his new cellmates began to persecute him. This ranged from verbal to physical intimidation. Once a week Fr. Calciu would kneel and pray through his liturgy. During this time the men would kick him, beat him, pull his hair out, scream and curse at him, and even urinate on him and make him eat his own faeces.

This continued week after week for over five months. They hadn't killed him, but they had abused him, beaten him very badly, and made his life a living hell. Then one day he knelt to pray as usual and the cell was oddly silent. He continued to pray, expecting the abuse to begin at any moment, but there was no screaming; no beating. He opened his eyes and found that the men were kneeling on the floor beside him, both of them weeping.

It was then they confessed that they had been commissioned to kill him, on a promise of being released from prison if they were successful. One of them said to Fr. Calciu,

"It didn't matter what we did to you, you just loved us. Neither of us has ever experienced love like this in our lives before."

He explained to them that it was beyond his capacity as a person to love unconditionally, but that the love of God flowed through him, and it was Christ's love they had experienced. He then led them both to faith in Christ in their prison cell. The very next day both men were removed from the cell and he never saw them again. Fr. Calciu told me that he thought they may have been executed because they didn't fulfil their mission.

* * *

Some of Fr. Calciu's meetings in the UK were in Essex, so he stayed with my parents for a short time. He came with his wife, Adrianna, who was an impish lady, full of fun, but couldn't speak a word of English. All she ever wanted to do was to go shopping with my mum, because she'd never seen stores full of goods. All the shops in Romania were empty.

Fr. Calcui got on really well with my dad and made himself at home with my parents. One thing I noticed was that when he arrived back at the house he would take off his priest's robes and sit wearing just his shirt and trousers. I had never known a priest do that. He knew how to relax!

Fr. Calcui was a very special man and became like a spiritual father to me. He loved the fact that I was a Christian involved in politics and he always encouraged me to keep doing what I was doing. The last time I saw him was at one of the US President's National Prayer Breakfasts. We met at my hotel in downtown Washington.

"You know, Merv," he told me. "I wish I was back in my prison cell."

"What do you mean?" I asked, taken aback by this statement."

"When I was in prison," he explained, "I had no choice but to throw myself into the abyss of God's love. That's all I could do. Now, I don't need God."

He was speaking rhetorically. He hadn't lost his faith. What he meant was, living in freedom in America, he didn't have to depend on God like he used to. In prison he had to trust God from day to day, and didn't know whether he would live or die. He was in a place of complete surrender. To that extent, he felt that his spiritual life was much more alive in adversity than it was in comfort. What a staggering thought.

I didn't see him again after that and a year or so later he died of cancer.

Whilst our theology differed in so many ways, Fr. Calcui was a tremendous influence on my life. He was an amazing man of God and I respected him greatly. My life has been richer for having known and loved him.

9. Back to Romania

The following year, I was invited to visit Romania again. CSI HQ were sending an undercover journalist from Switzerland to investigate the real state of religious freedom in the nation. David Atkinson had been invited to go out and act as the "official" face of the trip, and he asked me to join him. Knowing that we were planning to gather intelligence in a covert manner slightly worried me, although I knew there was no other way to do it. If I'm honest I was a little scared to go, yet knew in my heart that it was the right thing to do, so I agreed.

David had no problem getting a visa for Romania. His staff played the, "Surely you're not going to turn down a member of parliament?" card. I, on the other hand, had a great deal more difficulty. I was also in a tricky position because I'd agreed to go on the trip at the last minute and only had a few days in which to get a visa.

At the time I was living in Cambridgeshire and needed to take a trip into London to visit the Romanian embassy. I really needed to walk out with my visa in hand, there and then. I walked in and spoke to an officious looking lady behind a desk.

"Good morning. I'd like to get a visa to travel to Romania please."

"That's fine," she said. "Leave your passport with us. Come back in a week's time and we will tell you if your visa has been granted."

"I haven't got time for that," I said.

"Why not?"

"Because I'm going to Romania on Wednesday."

"Well, you are not going to Romania on Wednesday, because you can't have a visa," she stoically informed me.

"But I've got to have my visa," I persisted. "I need to go."

"Well, you can't have one!" she responded irritably.

It wasn't like me to dig my heels in and be stubborn, but I told her,

"Look, I live in Cambridgeshire, not London. I can't go away and come back in a week, because I need to go to Romania in a few days' time. I'm going to sit here in reception, and I'm not leaving until you give me my visa!"

The woman snorted her disapproval and looked down at her paperwork, ignoring me. I went and sat down. Every now and then she would look up, glare at me, and say,

"You can sit there all day, but you won't get a visa!!!"

I said, "OK, I'll sit here until you close!" at which she would sigh and get back to her paperwork. All the while I was thinking, "I'm going to have to give up and go in a minute. How can I get out of here without losing face?!"

A short while later, a smartly dressed man walked through the reception area. I wasn't sure if he was the ambassador, but if he wasn't then he was at least his number two, on his way to lunch. He glanced quizzically at me, so I jumped up and went over to speak to him.

"Excuse me!" I blurted out. "I've come for a visa."

"Oh, well you need to go and visit the desk," he said.

"I did," I replied, "but they want to keep my passport for a week and I really have to go to Romania next Wednesday."

"I see," he told me. "But we have to make the necessary checks, you understand, and that takes time."

This is what I'd feared. When I left Romania on the previous trip, the Religious Affairs Minister had told me I'd never be welcome in his country again. In addition, my old friend John Wildrianne, who travelled to Romania a lot, had told me he had been summoned to the

Romanian Embassy soon after my last trip and asked if he knew me! Would they join those dots? I guessed they would.

"I realise that," I said, "but the thing is, I really need to leave with a visa *today.*"

"But the lady has just told you," he persisted, "that you cannot get a visa today. You have to leave your passport here and come back in a week. That is the procedure."

"But," I ventured, "*you* could do it, couldn't you? *You* could grant my visa. I'll still be waiting here when you get back from lunch."

He looked at his watch, sighed, and with a resigned shake of his head, instructed his staff to rubber stamp my visa, then he personally signed it, just to get me off their premises.

* * *

On the day of our trip to Romania I made a mistake that could have cost us the whole trip. David and I had been given a list of the families of Christians who had been imprisoned. It gave their names and addresses, and the name of the person who was in prison.

I was at a loss to know where to keep this list. If it was amongst my baggage then it might be found by Romania immigration. It was a single side of A4, so I decided to slip it inside a copy of the Sunday Express newspaper I'd bought at Heathrow airport.

In Bucharest, David Atkinson cleared immigration ahead of me with no problem (he'd cleverly folded his A4 list of names and hidden it in his underpants)! Then I came up to the immigration officers and they began searching my bag. They immediately discovered my Bible, which put them on alert. Then, to my horror, one of them decided to shake out the pages of my newspaper. The list of names and addresses floated straight out and immediately their demeanours changed.

"Stay here. Don't move," one of the officers barked.

He disappeared and minutes later came back with a man who was obviously a more senior officer. The new man began to question me.

"Who are the people on this list?" he demanded.

"I'm going to visit them," I said.

"Why do you want to visit them? These people are enemies of the State of Romania," he declared.

"They're my family," I told him. "I'm just going to visit them."

Ignoring that, he told me, "You are going to come with me."

He was about to haul me away when a voice cut through the conversation.

"Where are you going with my friend?"

It was David Atkinson. He had been waiting around for ages for me to appear and had begun to worry, so he came to look for me. The senior officer said to David,

"Are you with him?"

"Yes."

So he arrested us both!

We were taken to a claustrophobic little room with no windows and harsh lighting and locked in. Officials came in and went out and questioned us for several hours. At one point a very senior military officer came in, judging by his uniform and the number of medals he had. He asked us the same questions as everyone else:

"Who are these people?" and "What is the purpose of your visit?"

He couldn't speak English, so he had to question us through an interpreter and frequently lost his temper and shouted loudly. I was amazed at David Atkinson's cool demeanour. Every time the officer lost his cool and shouted, David pulled a packet of Polo mints out of his pocket and offered him one – and each time he accepted and calmed down!

At one point I needed to go to the bathroom and had to be escorted there. Standing at the urinal, I literally had a guard on either side of me holding an automatic weapon. Talk about being under pressure! When I returned to the interrogation room, the mood was still belligerent.

"In two hours you will be put on a plane and thrown out of our country," the high ranking military official yelled.

This time David lost it, and there were no more Polo mints!

"I am a member of the British Parliament," he said. "If you refuse me entry to your country, tomorrow it will be in every newspaper. Everyone will know how the Romanian government really treats people."

Seething, the officials retreated and David and I were left alone in the room. We could hear a heated conversation outside, then suddenly it stopped. An official came back into the room and spoke as if nothing had happened.

"Right, you are free to go."

"What do you mean, we're free to go?" I asked hesitantly. "You said we would be put on the next plane home."

"No, you can stay," he told us, and with that we were ushered out of the airport, although they did keep a number of my personal belongings, including my Bible.

David and I caught a taxi to downtown Bucharest and found our hotel. First thing the following morning we made our way to the British Embassy. Because David was an MP, they needed to know that he had arrived in the country. At the Embassy we encountered the same scenario as the previous year, but this time with the Ambassador himself.

“Why have you come,” asked the Ambassador. “Please, just go home.”

“We can’t go home,” I told him. “We want to see the families of these Christians who are in prison, and pray with them.”

He pleaded with us for well over an hour.

“Please, I’m retiring in a week’s time. The last thing I need before I retire is a diplomatic incident!”

We told him that we appreciated the awkward position he was in, but the last thing we were going to do was be defeated by the Romanian government and turn around and go home. We’d come with a single purpose in mind and we were going to get it done. His last ditch effort was to tell us,

“Look, do you know that the wife of the Romanian Ambassador in London was arrested last week for shoplifting in Harrods and deported? She was kicked out of the UK and sent home. Now you two are here. This is just the excuse the authorities are looking for to retaliate and kick someone out of Romania.”

Needless to say we refused and there was nothing more he could say.

* * *

One of the people on our list was the leader of the Brethren movement in Romania. He had been imprisoned, so we knew we wouldn’t be able to see him, but we wanted to at least visit his family. David decided we should try and visit them that night.

We got into a taxi and headed for the address we’d been given. Of course, we were being followed, and the fact that it was after dark made it seem all the more sinister. We arrived in an area similar to where Father George Calciu lived – typical, featureless monolithic apartment blocks.

It wasn't easy to locate a precise address unless you knew roughly where it was to begin with, which we didn't. At the bottom of the apartment buildings were park-like settings with grass and trees. As David and I walked around trying to find the correct block, we were aware of *Securitate* men moving behind trees, or semi-concealed behind bushes. It was very intimidating.

In the lobby of each apartment block were the names of the people occupying the various flats. With no clear idea of which block we wanted, we had to check several. We would scan down the list of occupants, not find the name we were looking for, then have to move on.

Eventually, we came to a building with a dark lobby. The lightbulbs had been removed from their sockets, so we couldn't read the names on the list. We had a feeling this was deliberate. We were wondering what to do when a young man emerged from a ground floor apartment. He was a university student and could speak some English. He pulled a cigarette lighter from his pocket and held it up to the list on the wall. It was then that we could see the names had been removed from flat number we were looking for.

Sadly, we never got to see that family. It might sound as though this was a failure, a wasted evening, and that's the way it felt to us, as we came home pretty deflated. But several years later I learned that it wasn't the disaster we had feared. I was invited to speak at a large event organised by the Romanian Evangelical Alliance. It was held in a very large hall, holding 8,000 people, where Ceaușescu had so often addressed the Communist Party faithful. It was a great privilege to speak, especially as I got to share a platform with the great, but by this time very frail, Richard Wurmbrand.

Backstage, I was introduced to a man who was a leader in the Brethren movement and someone told me he had been in prison. I told him,

"Several years ago, myself and David Atkinson – a member of Parliament in Britain – tried to visit the family of a Brethren leader who was in prison."

His face immediately lit up.

"It was me!" he exclaimed.

He went on to explain that even though we hadn't been able to see his family, the authorities were well aware that we had tried hard to find them. As a result they felt the heat was on and a short while later they released him.

"But I never knew who the people who came were," he said.

After that we hugged and it was very emotional.

I learned another important lesson on that visit. Even though David and I had returned to our hotel that night frustrated and somewhat downhearted, God was still working behind the scenes. It was amazing to hear of the events that had been triggered simply because we had *tried* to visit.

* * *

David Atkinson stayed one more night in Romania and then had to fly back to the UK. I stayed on with the Swiss journalist and decided to go and visit Paul Negrut in Oradea, who I'd met the previous year.

I found Paul's address and travelled to his house. He greeted me warmly and, like so many others living under the communist regime, immediately put on some loud music so that our conversation couldn't be overheard.

Paul told me of the miraculous ways in which God had protected and preserved the lives of him and his family. Just a few weeks earlier they had held a birthday party for his oldest daughter, who was in her early teens. Lots of friends and family were invited over. The party went well and everyone had a great time. At the end, as Paul said goodbye to the last few guests leaving the house, he noticed something outside. There was a cable attached to the metal guttering, which stretched away around a corner. He followed it as it led away into some trees and he eventually found that it was attached to an electricity pylon. All the time the party had been in full swing, the entire house had been live. He wasn't sure whether, miraculously, no one had touched an outside wall, or whether God had simply caused it to fail. He had many similar stories of divine intervention.

Years later came a chilling postscript to this story...

Paul Negrut called to tell me he would be visiting London and asked to meet up. When we eventually met in a small café near Westminster he looked worried. He told me that recently the government had released the historic *Securitate* files and for the first time people could learn about the information the communist regime had held about them.

"I thought I would go and have a look at the files," he told me, "and they had an impressive file on you Merv – as an enemy of the State."

"That doesn't surprise me," I told him.

"But then I discovered something that has turned my world upside down," he said, suddenly grave.

Paul was one of two pastors of Second Baptist church in Oradea. Paul and his fellow pastor were a great double act in leading the church and had a very close personal relationship.

"Of course, I read my own file, then the file of my co-leader," he said. "This is when I discovered that he had been working for the *Securitate* the entire time we worked together."

I was shocked.

"Worse than that," Paul continued, "it was he who ordered my house to be wired to the electricity pylon before my daughter's birthday party."

With tears in his eyes he told me,

"Merv, he was the *only* person I trusted in Romania."

The two of them had attended the same university in Bucharest, so had known each other for many years. Then this guy had turned up at Paul's church and given an incredible, compelling testimony of his conversion. They became great friends after that. Now, Paul was forced to question whether his fellow pastor had been planted by the *Securitate* and had made up his conversion testimony; or whether his conversion had been genuine and he had been recruited later, making the decision to betray his friend and fellow minister. So many questions.

* * *

I had two hair-raising experiences right at the end of this particular trip. After visiting Paul in Oradea, the Swiss journalist and I set out to travel back to Bucharest by train. At the train station I spotted a man with a familiar face – a *Securitate* operative who had followed me many times. He got on the train with us and sat nearby. I noticed that he had a bottle of beer with him, and judging by his behaviour it was by no means his first that day. At one point my colleague stepped into the corridor to go to the bathroom and when he came back I noticed the *Securitate* guy approach him.

The not-so-secret policeman threw his arm around the reporter and began chatting to him in English like an amiable drunk. As he was doing so, I saw him casually drop some jewellery into my friend's pocket. As soon as I saw this I jumped up.

"Hey! I saw what you did then. You slipped something in his pocket! Why have you done that?"

The man tried to bluff his way out of it.

"What? What?"

"I saw you put that in his pocket."

"It's a gift – a gift for my friend here!" he exclaimed.

"You take that out of his pocket and go," I insisted.

He shrugged his shoulders, retrieved the jewellery and retreated. It was a known tactic of the *Securitate.* If they didn't have anything on you, they would plant evidence then accuse you of some crime. Fortunately, I managed to foil this attempt.

The second incident occurred after I'd checked out of my hotel and was on my way to catch my flight home. I jumped into a waiting taxi and asked for the international airport. Although my trips to Romania were so valuable in enabling me to meet and encourage persecuted believers, I always felt a sense of relief when I managed to leave the country and travel home without being harassed or detained. So I was sitting in the taxi thinking, "Great, I'm on my way home."

In order to get to the international airport, you had to drive past the smaller national airport. I was familiar with the route, but just before the smaller airport, we found ourselves stopped at a police roadblock. The road to the international airport was completely shut off.

My taxi driver was clearly displeased about this. He wound down his window and began a heated conversation with a police officer. The last thing I wanted to do was to draw attention to myself, but the heated conversation escalated into a full-on shouting match. I didn't know what they were saying because it was all in Romanian. The argument went on for some time until the policeman reluctantly decided to allow us through the roadblock. The taxi driver had apparently persuaded the policeman that we were only going to the National Airport, one hundred yards from the junction.

However, the taxi driver ignored the right turn, put his foot down and we sped off. I knew something was very wrong as I soon noticed that there was no other traffic on the stretch of road leading to the international airport. Nothing coming either way. What I didn't know then, was that the Romanian President had landed at the airport and his entourage were escorting him back to his headquarters.

We hurtled down this empty road, but it wasn't empty for long. Soon, over the horizon towards us came a huge cavalcade. It was the President's car, around 20 other cars, and at least 50 motorcycle outriders. I had never seen anything like it. The horrified taxi driver slammed on the brakes and pulled onto the side of the road. Both of us sat there, paralysed, and looked out of the window as government vehicles passed us, one after the other.

The driver waited until the whole procession had passed, then I heard him exclaim as he looked in his rear view mirror. I looked around and saw that a number of police cars had peeled off from the cavalcade and were now heading in our direction. Before I had chance to open my mouth my driver had hit the gas and he left the scene as though initiating a car chase. Instead of getting back on the carriageway, he decided to take the scenic route and went off-road!

The taxi driver bumped up the curb and drove straight into a field, taking the most direct route to the airport. We cut across this field, into a narrow lane, then straight into another field. He even smashed through a small fence in an effort to keep the police off his tail. Somehow he successfully evaded capture and, as we sped into the airport drop zone, the taxi driver yelled,

"50 Leu please sir!"

I literally threw the money at him, grabbed my bag and ran.

Mum and Dad - Betty and Syd

Meg and me 1952!

Dad and Grandma Lily (CSI calendar on the wall)

Romania 1985, From Left to Right: Justin Fashanu, Mary McDermott (Noonan), me, Congressman Chris Smith

Moscow 1988: Congressman Robert Pittenger, Interpreter, Mike Farris, me, Steve Snyder, David Amess MP, Scott Flipse, Mrs Carolyn Wolf, Congressman Frank Wolf

London 1990: Konstantin Kharchev (Soviet Minister for Religious Affairs), Lord Archer (former Solicitor General), David Atkinson MP (co-founder of CSW), me, Rev John Wildrianne, (CSW Deputy Chairman)

Wendy and me on our wedding day

Wendy, me Seth and Vix

Wendy and me with Fr George Calciu

Me with Field Marshal Abdel Fattah el Sisi
(a few days before he declared his candidacy for Egyptian Presidency)

John Glen MP, me, Sir Jeffrey Donaldson MP, Jim Shannon MP
outside Egyptian Presidency

Taking my opportunity to engage Prime Minister David Cameron about the notorious Pakistani Blasphemy Laws - my good friend Archbishop Angaelos looks on

One of my last pictures with my dear friend Stu. Seen here with friends and CSW supporters Julian and Marina Speroni and their children Thiago and Isabella

Lalish, Nr Sinjar, Iraq: Yazidi Spiritual Leader, Baba Sheikh, Congressman Frank Wolf and me discussing the plight of 3,000 Yazidi girls, who were still missing following capture by ISIS

Me, Congressman Frank Wolf, Abby Berg and Todd Chasteen
in Samaritan's Purse Field Hospital, Mosul, Iraq

Seth with villagers in Asso, Southern Kaduna, 2017

10. Revolution

The year was 1989 and there was a revolution taking place in Romania. It was just one of a wave of revolutions that began in Poland and swept across central and eastern Europe that year in an effort to overthrow communist rule. In Romania it culminated in the show trial and execution of Nicolae Ceauşescu and his wife, Elena, on Christmas Day.

I hadn't been back to Romania since my last visit in 1986, but I had kept in close contact with Paul Negrut. I remember one particular night I felt prompted to phone Paul. I had no real reason to, I just felt an urge to speak with him. I called and we chatted for several minutes. He couldn't say a great deal, and I knew this was because his home phone was bugged and conversations were being monitored. A few years later, however, he told me that the phone call had been timely and meant a lot.

That day his daughter had come home from school and told Paul she didn't want to be a Christian any more. It had an adverse effect on her life at school and she was bullied not only by the students, but the teachers too.

The school insisted on Christians being singled out and ridiculed, so on her exercise books it stated her name, then underneath said "Daughter of the Baptist preacher". All her teachers had told her that there were no other Christians anywhere in the world and that the Bible was a book of fables. Paul had been trying to talk this through with his daughter when I called. When he came off the phone he told her,

"That was a man who is a Christian from another country, and his job is to speak up for other Christians all over the world."

She was amazed by this and it was a real turning point in her faith. Once again, it was just a small, seemingly insignificant thing that made a big difference.

* * *

The revolution took place in the December of 1989 and I visited there the following June. During the tumultuous months that followed an interim government led by President Iliescu set about administrating the nation.

I stayed in the same hotel where I'd stayed previously, which was located on University Square. Since December of the previous year the square had been controlled by students staging a sit-in, and they were still there in June. The square was effectively closed, no traffic could get into it since it was occupied by hundreds of tents housing thousands of protestors. Day and night they broadcast their protests via loudspeakers and after I'd settled into my room I thought, "I'm not going to get much sleep tonight."

I rose early the next day, as I was due to go and visit some orphanages. As I was getting ready in my room, I heard tremendous popping and cracking sounds coming from outside. My immediate thought was, "That sounds like fireworks." I went over to the window and peered out. To my horror I saw that the square was surrounded by armed officers. I couldn't tell whether they were police or army, but they were indiscriminately firing into the centre of the protestors. People screamed and ran in all directions. This was around 5.00am.

By the time I met my friends in the hotel lobby at 7.00am – and with some difficulty relayed to them the horrific scenes I'd witnessed – the square was completely deserted. Not only that, but all the tents had been cleared away, the banners that protestors had draped over buildings removed, and even the streets washed to remove any trace of blood. It was as though the protest had never happened, yet I knew many people had been killed.

It turned out that this wasn't the only terrible thing I'd witness this day. We decided to continue with the orphanage visit. There I witnessed some of the most horrific conditions I've ever seen children having to live in. Babies were lying on putrid mattresses soaked in months of their own urine. All of the children had their heads shaved to prevent them from getting lice. The nurses, allegedly there to care for the children, completely ignored them and did nothing to improve their condition or quality of life.

In the garden the children were kept like animals in a large cage and the law of the jungle prevailed. I saw one boy of around 15, walk up behind a little boy of 5 or 6, and bang him repeatedly on the head with his drinking mug. While this was happening, the staff were stood in the corner of the room, chatting, joking and laughing, completely oblivious. I noticed that the little boy being hit had tears rolling down his cheeks, but he never uttered a word or cried out. Immediately I shouted out to the bigger boy to stop. I said to our interpreter,

"That's terrible. But why didn't that small boy make any noise or shout out?"

"Because children only cry out in order to get attention," he explained ruefully, "and the boy knows that he won't get any attention here."

* * *

When we returned to our hotel that evening, all hell broke out in Bucharest. The sound of further gunfire filled the air and helicopters were flying low over our hotel. Cars and even buses and lorries had been turned over and set on fire. Naturally, we felt very unsafe staying in the hotel and wondered what we could do. Fortunately, the young man who had been driving us around was a Christian and suggested we could stay in his sister's apartment on the edge of town, since she was away in Germany at that time.

The next morning, for reasons that escape me now, the young man drove me back into the centre of Bucharest on the way to the airport. The civil unrest was still at its height and once more University Square was filling up with protestors. This time President Illiescu called on the coal miners for hired muscle to quell the protests. Miners, who looked like they'd literally come straight from the pit, thronged in the square wielding batons. They were beating protestors and trying to disperse them. Worse still, they were pulling people from their cars and beating them. Unfortunately, my nervous young driver took a wrong turn that led us down a dead end street. He executed a hasty three-point turn, but there was no way out of this street except through the miners. As we tried to drive away, a group came at us with batons and began battering the car. It was a terrifying experience, but somehow we managed to escape without being dragged from the vehicle. Once again, I was more than relieved when I was on my plane, leaving the tarmac at Bucharest airport.

A postscript to this story happened in 2016 when I visited my old friend Frank Wolf in Congress.

"Come in, Merv," he said. 'I've got somebody here you should meet."

The man in Frank's office was the leader of the student protests in University Square in 1990, and he was amazed when I told him that I had witnessed the killings on the morning their camp was broken up.

* * *

After this I visited Romania a couple more times in 1992 and 1993. For one of those trips Paul Negrut asked me to bring another British politician with me, to speak at an Evangelical Alliance gathering.

"How about Jonathan Aitken," he suggested.

"Jonathan Aitken? I'm not aware that he's a Christian politician," I told him.

"But he came and spoke last year," Paul said.

I was very surprised by this and thought that perhaps Jonathan hadn't known what it was he'd agreed to attend! Rather than approach him, however, I opted to take Lord Barry Ashbourne with me. He was a hereditary peer and sat in the House of Lords; he was also a full on Charismatic Christian. I used to meet with him regularly as a prayer partner. I remember on one occasion him phoning me, asking to meet up, but I couldn't do it because I was feeling unwell.

"Sorry, Barry, I can't see you this afternoon, I'm not feeling well."

"It's okay old boy," he told me, "I'll pray for you."

Then he began speaking in tongues very loudly down the telephone. When he'd finished I asked him,

"Where are you at the moment?"

"Oh, I'm in the central lobby," he replied.

This, of course, is the core of the Palace of Westminster – an incredibly busy thoroughfare, where the corridors from the Lords, Commons and Westminster Hall all converge. This made me smile a lot!

The purpose of the trip to Romania this time was to attend the opening of the newly built Oradea Second Baptist Church and to visit the Christian university connected to it. This was a sign of how things had changed over the years. A Christian university would have been unthinkable in the Romania I had first visited.

This trip was still not without its drama, however. I said a few words at the event and brought my greetings, then sat down on the front row. Some hymns were sung and, during one of them, a guy suddenly leapt onto the stage and produced a huge knife. People froze as he grabbed hold of one of the pastors of the church. The whole time he was ranting, though I couldn't understand what he was saying. Then one of the other pastors bravely stepped forward, put his arm around the man, and peeled him away. I could see him talking calmly to the man and, gradually, the man lowered his knife. The pastor took it away from him and the man was escorted out.

Sadly, that was my last visit to Romania, but I'm sure I will visit there again someday. One lovely thing was that Paul Negrut came to live in London for a while, to study at the London School of Theology. He was in the UK when I got married to Wendy, and so was able to preach at our wedding, which was really special for us. Paul is now the Rector of the Emmanuel Christian University and I still see him from time to time, often in Washington DC, when we both attend the US National Prayer Breakfast.

11. Russia

After meeting US congressman Frank Wolf on my very first trip to Romania, we became good friends and a few years later I travelled with Frank to Russia.

It was 1987, an era of huge political change. President Mikhail Gorbachev had begun using the phrase *glasnost* as his political slogan. In Russian glasnost literally means "publicity" but was interpreted as "openness and transparency". The origins of the phrase go all the way back to 1965 and the Soviet civil rights movement.

Margaret Thatcher was in power in Downing Street and famously said, "I like Mr Gorbachev. We can do business together..." in an interview with BBC journalist John Cole. In the December of that year, US President Ronald Reagan held a summit with Gorbachev in Washington. These were ground-breaking events in the midst of the Cold War era.

But despite these political breakthroughs, there were still countless Christians in Russia being persecuted for their faith – hence the need to visit and raise awareness. Accompanying me from the UK was David Amess. At the time David was the MP for Basildon. Now Sir David Amess, he is the MP for Southend West.

The purpose of our trip was to try and meet with believers who had been imprisoned or exiled. There were two high profile individuals in particular we wanted to find out about: Alexander Ogorodnikov and Father Gleb Yakunin. Both these men had been subject to imprisonment and we had campaigned for them to be released. We wanted to find out what their current situation was. Beyond this, our trip was a fact-finding mission. Despite the national narrative of "openness and transparency", the ordinary citizens of Russia didn't really know what that meant. We wanted to uncover the real state of affairs for people of faith. We wanted to pray with and encourage believers and let those in prison know we were trying to get in to see them.

Father Gleb Yakunin was a Russian Orthodox priest who had campaigned vigorously on human rights issues. He was born into a Christian family in Moscow, lost his faith at the age of 15, but found his way again spiritually and went on to become extremely influential. He worked tirelessly to bring the plight of the persecuted Church to the attention of the free Church and political powers around the world.

Fr. Gleb had written an open letter to the World Council of Churches. Bear in mind that in the late 80s, the senior leadership of the Russian Orthodox Church were forced to work hand in glove with the Communist government. Fr. Gleb's letter pleaded for clarity and truth, since the government insisted that there was religious freedom in Russia. He asked the council of churches to do all of the things that we do routinely today as CSW – to organise prayer, to advocate for prisoners by lobbying the authorities, and to write letters of support and encouragement to those in prison. Despite his pleas, however, he was largely ignored, and spent a number of years in prison and later in exile.

We'd heard that Fr. Gleb had recently been released and was living in an apartment that we managed to track down, and it was arranged that a group of us would go and visit him.

Frank Wolf and his staffer, Scott Flipse (who has continued to work for religious freedom, having had a career spanning the United States Commission on Religious Freedom, and at the time of writing is serving as a senior staffer with Congressman Chris Smith) travelled in a car specially laid on by the US Embassy. David Amess and I had to find our own way there. In those days, if you wanted to go anywhere in Moscow, you simply stood on the pavement and stuck out your thumb. Whether they were officially licensed or not, any car stopped and gave you a lift if you paid them!

Using this method, David and I stood in the street and flagged down a large black car, which immediately pulled over. It had privacy screens in the back which were pulled up and, truthfully I should have suspected something right away. Having established that we were British "tourists", the driver asked in broken English,

"Where do you want to go?"

We gave him the address and off we went. As we drove, David shuffled uncomfortably in his seat and looked behind him. He discovered he was half-sitting on a large blue light, intended to be placed on top of the car. It was then that I realised we'd pulled over a KGB car!

Frank Wolf in the US Embassy car had arrived at the apartment block shortly before us. Moments later our KGB car turned up and the Americans scuttled around looking guilty. Frank couldn't believe his eyes when the doors opened and we emerged from the back!

Fr. Gleb lived in a typically austere, small dingy apartment. We had taken a gift to give him – a Russian Bible – which he was delighted with, and I remember him just kissing the Bible over and over throughout our visit.

Bibles were extremely scarce in Russia then. Something that struck me time and again whilst visiting Christian families on this trip was how they all had scraps of paper with small portions of the Bible copied out. Some of the writing on these bits of paper was very feint because they were ninth or tenth generation carbon copies, so the quality was very poor. Yet they were the Christians' most treasured possessions. They placed immense value on the Word of God.

We talked with Fr. Gleb through an interpreter and it was an inspirational and very moving meeting. He told us about the many cards and letters of support he had received and explained just how much they had meant to him. Whilst he had been imprisoned, then exiled, God had used these simple communications to remind him he had not been forgotten.

* * *

Alexander Ogorodnikov was a peace activist and the founder of a number of Russian humanitarian organisations. Although his father was a member of the Communist Party, his grandmother secretly had him baptised. He was targeted as an "enemy of the State" because he refused to agree with the Soviet scientific doctrine on the eradication of religious belief. Alexander further clashed with the authorities because he had been involved in running soup kitchens for the poor, and working in the community in the name of Christianity had been outlawed. I thought it might be very difficult to visit him, much as it had been difficult to see people in Romania, but we did manage to meet and pray with him, even though it was on a street corner. This was the *glasnost* era and things had relaxed slightly.

We also met with various officials from the Soviet leadership. Konstantin Kharchev was the Head of the Religious Affairs Bureau and a member of the Politburo – the highest policy-making government department of the Communist Party. We met at his office. I don't know what made me say it, but during the meeting I felt compelled to ask him bluntly,

"Mr Kharchev, I wonder if you would give me official permission to bring one million Bibles into Russia?"

The Bible was a banned book and I anticipated a frosty reaction, but I got a surprise.

"Yes," he replied without hesitation.

Taken aback, my mind raced.

First of all, why has he said yes? And second, where on earth will I get a million Bibles from?!

Later, when I'd returned to the UK, I followed up on the conversation, writing to Kharchev, and in due course received his reply confirming that I indeed had permission to import and distribute one million copies of the Bible. (The letter was written in Russian – I had to get it translated). During the following year, one million New Testaments were sent with the help of the Bible Society and Open Doors.

I was puzzled as to why Kharchev had so readily granted permission for this to happen, but 18 months later I got the answer.

Kharchev came on an official visit to London. He informed David Amess about the visit, who told me, and we arranged to meet him. The first thing he said to me was,

"Thank you for sending the Bibles, but you only sent half the Bible!"

"Ah, yes," I said. "It was the New Testament."

"Would you like permission to send a further one million Bibles?" he said. "But this time, you must send the whole Bible."

"That would be wonderful," I told him, "but I don't understand. You're a communist and an atheist. Why are you suddenly opening your doors to the Bible?"

"You are right," he responded. "I am an atheist and I want to see Christianity wiped out in Russia."

"So why do you want the Bibles then?"

"The Bible has been banned throughout Communist rule," he explained. "We thought that by banning the Bible, the Church would disappear. But it hasn't. It has gone underground and instead of destroying the Church, banning the Bible has caused it to grow."

His logic began to dawn on me.

"I come to your country, or America," he continued, "and in your bookstores I can buy 40 different versions of the Bible if I want to.

Every hotel room I stay in has a Bible in the drawer. Despite this, your churches are empty."

His thought process was: make the Bible as widely available as possible and the Church will become complacent and begin to wither away. Flood the market and the Church will die. It was a salutary lesson to learn from an atheist, but I felt there was some truth to it.

A wonderful postscript to this story, is that I learned just this year that Konstantin Kharchev has become a Christian and names the now deceased Pentecostal leader Ivan Fedetov (imprisoned under the Soviet Leadership) as his teacher!

* * *

One evening during our visit to Moscow we were all invited to an official dinner at the residence of the US Ambassador. As in many other official meetings, I recall Frank Wolf speaking to the Russian dignitaries present very loudly and bluntly about the Christians who were suffering persecution in prison. Frank was never afraid to challenge officials and took every opportunity to put them on the spot.

Lots of prominent people had been invited to the dinner and I found myself sitting next to a very senior Archbishop of the Orthodox church. We chatted about all sorts of things and he spoke to me in perfect English. At one point I took the plunge and asked him point blank whether the Church was speaking up for an imprisoned Orthodox Deacon, Vladimir Rusak, who we were campaigning for.

"What are you doing about Vladimir?" I said.

"Pardon?" he responded.

"What representations are you making to the government on behalf of Vladimir?" I added for clarification, in case he'd misunderstood me.

"Pardon?" he said again.

I repeated everything I'd said and he simply replied,

"Sorry, no speak English."

With that, he turned his back towards me and spoke to the person on the other side of him in Russian for the rest of the evening. Despite glasnost and all the talk of tolerance and openness, here was a microcosm of the *real* situation. People were still afraid to speak; still afraid to stand up for the rights of others.

Our trip ended with a complication at Moscow airport. David Amess lived in Basildon at the time, just down the road from me in Grays, Essex. I had picked him up to drive us to Heathrow airport at the beginning of our trip and handed him his plane tickets. In those days, you were given a small "book" of tickets, like coupons, which contained both the outgoing and return flight tickets. The idea was to rip off the outgoing ticket and save the book for the return flight. Arriving at the airport David said to me,

"Can I have my ticket home please Merv."

"I gave you your ticket, David," I said.

"No, you didn't. You only gave me my ticket out here," he replied.

"No, the book I gave you in Basildon had *both* tickets in it," I explained. "Where is it?"

"Oh, well, I threw it in the bin at the hotel," he told me.

A big scene ensued at the airport as we tried to sort things out. The airport authorities were unsympathetic and uncooperative. Things escalated to the point where Frank Wolf weighed in and told them,

"Now look, I'm a member of the US Congress and this man is a member of the British Parliament!"

The inscrutable airport official didn't bat an eyelid and responded,

"I don't care who you are. He is not travelling without a ticket."

Eventually, we managed to persuade him to let David travel, but not before we'd paid £100 indemnity charge, in case someone else turned up to claim the seat.

Despite many years of relative religious freedom Russia continues to be a difficult place for Christians to live. In July 2016, President Putin approved a package of "anti-terrorism" laws that included tighter restrictions on missionary activity and evangelism. This included a ban on sharing faith in homes, online, and anywhere apart from officially recognised church buildings.

12. Wendy

I never really had any girlfriends at school, though I secretly liked several. There was Ruth; there was Liz; then there was Glenda – or slender Glenda as everyone called her! I had friends who were girls, but I had never had a proper girlfriend until much later.

Each year, from 1972 until 1992 when I married Wendy, I would attend the annual Assembles of God conference in Minehead. Being the super-spiritual person that I am, the main reason I wanted to go was in order to meet girls! I would hang out with groups of girls, but I could never pluck up the courage to ask anyone out.

After several years of this, one year, on the very last day of the conference, I found the courage to speak to a girl and ask her whether she'd like to go out with me. She sweetly said that she would. It turned out, however, that she lived in the north east, while I lived in Essex. Perhaps the relationship was doomed from the start. Nevertheless, we wrote to each other each week. I never actually went to see her, we just wrote letters, and I sent her some flowers on her birthday. We arranged to meet at the next AoG conference, so effectively we'd been pen friends for a year.

When conference time came around, we arranged to meet in the café area of the venue. This might sound harsh, but I walked into the café that day, spotted her sitting with her friends, and thought, "Oh no, she's not how I remember her. I'm not sure I really fancy her after all!"

I was in a quandary and made a split-second decision to keep my head down and quietly walk by, but she spotted me and called out.

"Oh, Merv! Merv!"

"Oh, hi! I didn't see you there..."

To cut a long story short, we spent an awkward week in each other's company and any hint of a romance fizzled out there and then.

For years after that I had girlfriends on and off, but none of the relationships really worked out and I was dumped and did the dumping in equal measure. This was mainly during my 20s. In my 30s I only really had one relationship that didn't work out. But without doubt, my best friend was Jacquie Daly from Slough, who I met at a youth camp when I was 24 and she was still in her teens. Although there was never any real romance, we remained in touch and she was my regular "date" when I needed to take a girl anywhere! We jokingly made a pact that if I wasn't married by the time I reached 40 she and I would marry.

I was now approaching 40 and though I really wanted to get married and settle down, I began to think, "Nothing is working out. Maybe God doesn't want me to be married?"

CSW was growing and I knew that this was the main thing God had called me to do in life. I thought "Maybe I just better get on with this and forget about trying to find a partner."

After having moved for a while to live in Newmarket, working for *Sweet'n Low*, I had now returned to Grays, and although I attended another church, on occasions I would visit my parent's church for a change of scenery. It was here that I first saw Wendy, who is now my wife. I was immediately attracted to her and thought, "Wow, who is that?" Wendy, a Welsh girl from Merthyr, had been in a marriage which ended several years previously, and she had a six-year old daughter, Victoria.

My parents had got to know Wendy quite well and had really befriended her and Victoria.

At this time I was the chairman of the local Bible Society action group, and Dad was secretary of the group too. One day, after mowing his lawn for him, I said,

"Dad, do you think it would be good to have someone else from your church sit on the action group, besides you."

"Hmm, that's a really good idea," he said.

"I was thinking that Welsh girl would be ideal," I told him.

"Wendy, you mean?"

"Yeah, Wendy. Why don't you ask her to be on the committee?"

"Yes, I will," he said. "I think she'd be very good."

So, I managed to engineer us spending a bit more time together.

Before she joined the committee the Bible Society put on a church event – a kind of fun evening where we played a Bible version of the old TV programme *Call My Bluff*. For the uninitiated, three people gave definitions of words, only one of which was the true meaning; the others were false and the audience had to guess the true meaning. We did this with biblical words and I was one of the panel. None of my definitions were the real ones – I just made up convincing sounding explanations off the top of my head. Wendy was taken in by me every single time and thought that I had the right answer, but I was bluffing each time!

That was the beginning of us getting to know each other. But then I thought, "Well, what do I do about this, Lord, to take it further?" I really liked Wendy and prayed about it a lot. "If this is right God, you've got to make it happen." I didn't want another stalled relationship.

Call me a schemer, but the following plan suddenly occurred to me – a way of letting Wendy know how I felt about her. You may recall from an earlier chapter the lady who played the piano at our youth meetings, who had the misfortune of having a dead cat put in her piano by some Hell's Angels. I had known her since a child, and she was a friend, but I knew that on occasion she could be, how can I put it, less than discreet. Keeping secrets was not necessarily her forte. So,

I decided to go and have a chat with her.

“Could I have a chat with you?” I asked her. “There’s something I really need to talk about.”

“Of course,” she said, all ears.

“You know Wendy in your church,” I said.

“Yes.”

“Do you happen to know if she’s going out with anyone?”

“I don’t think so,” she said. “Why, are you interested?”

“Oh, well, err, don’t say anything…”

“Oh no, of course not!”

Needless to say, it wasn’t long before she spoke to Wendy and told her, “I know someone who fancies you!” which of course I knew full well would happen and is why I spoke to her in the first place!

This was around October time and although letting her know how I felt was a start, nothing much happened and I found myself praying,

“Lord, please give me a positive sign before Christmas that this is going somewhere or I’ll just forget all about it.”

Christmas Eve came and I was on my way home from the chip shop thinking to myself, “Oh well, that prayer hasn’t been answered.” When I got in, however, I found a message from my dad on my answer machine. Because I travelled so much, if I ever needed something delivered I sent it to my parents’ house, and Dad’s message told me that a computer I’d ordered had arrived. “That’s great,” I thought, “I can get it set up over Christmas.”

I later discovered that Wendy and her daughter, Victoria, had been visiting my parents when the package arrived and she’d asked who it was for. When my dad told her it was for me, she told him that she'd really like to see my computer some time (personal computers were relatively rare in 1991). Dad relayed this information to me and I thought, "Well, that's a sign. If she wanted to stay clear of me, she wouldn't want to come and visit."

On Christmas Day I went to church with my parents, and when Wendy arrived she greeted my mum and dad with a kiss. I cheekily added, "Where's mine?!" After the service we sat and chatted and I invited Wendy around to my house to see the computer. She came and visited my home on a day that Victoria was visiting her father's family, and I asked her what she was doing on New Year's Eve. She explained that a youth event had been planned, but she didn't really want to go to it.

"Oh, well would you like to go out for a meal with me then?" I ventured.

"Well, that might be difficult as Victoria will be back home, so why don't you come round to my house and I'll cook something for you?" she replied.

"That would be great," I told her.

Having agreed to go, I was then really nervous about it. I've already mentioned what a fussy eater I am, so I began to worry. "What if she cooks me something I can't eat? How embarrassing will that be?"

Wendy lived in an apartment block and when I arrived on New Year's Eve, she opened the door and told me,

"Oh, I haven't even started cooking yet!"

"Oh, never mind," I said. "Let's have an Indian takeaway shall we?"

"That would be really nice," she said. "Are you sure?"

"Quite sure!"

That evening started a tradition and every New Year's Eve since we have an Indian takeaway.

We got on wonderfully and what I remember most from that night was that we both said if we were going to go out with a person – theoretically speaking – it would have to mean marriage eventually. We were both at a point in our lives where we didn't want just another relationship as girlfriend/boyfriend.

At midnight we went out onto her little balcony which overlooked the Thames, as all the boats on the river would blow their horns at New Year. Wendy had some party poppers and handed one to me. It was the first time I'd ever let off a party popper and I held it the wrong way around, which resulted in me burning my hand – what an embarrassment!

The next day we went to the cinema together and I took her home afterwards. We chatted late into the evening and eventually I blurted out,

"Well, are you going to go out with me or not?"

"Well, I want to know more about you first," she said. "Tell me your testimony. I've heard a few things about you. My friend, Richard (the Hell's Angel who got saved), told me to steer clear of you!"

I explained to her that I'd had quite a few failed relationships, but I wasn't the same person any more. She listened intently, then said,

"OK, but before you go, let's pray together."

We did and it was great. We had a wonderful connection.

We got engaged on Valentine's Day. We were out walking around the town and I said to Wendy,

"Oh, let's just pop in here a minute."

It was a jeweller's store and I immediately knelt down and proposed to her in the shop. I don't know whether the store manager had seen this a hundred times before, but he wasn't impressed, and Wendy was extremely embarrassed!

This little incident almost put Wendy off me forever, but she graciously persevered and shortly afterwards took me to her mothers in Reading. This was an awkward meeting, to say the least. Apart from Wendy's mum, Pat, there were also two of her sisters and a chap called George Dunn, who was later to become my brother-in-law. There I was, surrounded by these ladies (and George), feeling a bit like I was being interrogated. At one point, when Wendy announced that we were going to get married, her mum immediately leapt up and ran screaming into the kitchen, followed by Wendy's sisters and wailing,

"OH NO! IT'S TOO SOON, YOU'VE ONLY KNOWN EACH OTHER A MONTH!"

I was left with George, sitting in the living room, staring into my teacup, hoping the ground would swallow me up. George quietly got up and came over to shake my hand.

"Oh, well, congratulations old chap!"

Our next job was to tell my parents we were setting a date for our wedding. I was bit nervous about this – not because I had any doubts they'd be happy about our plans, but because my dad had a weak heart by this time. When we'd told him about our engagement on Valentine's Day, he'd reacted by having serious palpitations and a minor heart attack. He ended up in hospital and explained later that it was probably because he had been so excited. This worried me greatly. However, we gave him our news and he seemed fine.

The last time I saw my dad was when I popped round to see him just before I was due to go away for the weekend to the annual CSW vision building event at the IBTI in Burgess Hill. We were chatting and Mum was in the garden hanging out the washing. Dad told me that he and Mum wanted to pay at least half the cost of our wedding.

"I just want to tell you that I know you're doing the right thing," he told me, and gave me his blessing. He really loved Wendy.

By now he was suffering with swelling in his legs and had been referred to a doctor at St Bart's hospital.

"Are you going to be alright, Dad?" I asked him.

"Oh yes," he said. "The doctor has prescribed me some tablets and everything's fine. By the time you get back I'll be as right as rain."

I drove down to the IBTI that Friday night and after all the sessions had finished, John Wildrianne invited me and my pal Franklin Evans up to his apartment for a nightcap. Around midnight his phone began ringing, which was unusual. Before John had answered it, I instinctively knew that Dad had passed away. John picked up then listened.

"Oh, yes, he's here. I'll get him. Merv, it's your aunt…"

I was always close to my dad and loved him very much. In that moment I regretted not having told him more often just how much. I would like to have told him how much he impacted my life by his example. I recalled the time Dad came along to a CSW event being held in Westminster. Afterwards he said to me,

"You really reminded me of my dad tonight, Merv," which was a big thing for him to say, and for me to hear (remember, my grandad was my hero).

"My dad was just like you. He knew all the important people and was comfortable with them, and with making speeches. I'm really proud of you!"

My dad died at the end of February and Wendy and I married on October 31, 1992. A very special time indeed, tinged with sadness that my dad wasn't there to share our happiness.

Incidentally, after telling our parents we were getting married, I thought I'd better call my friend Jacquie to tell her the news. It was just a few weeks before my 40th birthday. Believe it or not, when she answered the phone she said, "I suppose you've called to say you're getting married?" Jacquie and I have remained firm friends over the years, and Wendy and I regularly meet up with her and her husband John for dinner.

Victoria was six and half when Wendy and I began going out and seven by the time we got married. She wanted to call me Dad even before we were married and decided to take the surname Thomas in due course.

Like many teenagers, Victoria had her rebellious years, and stopped going to church with us from about the age of twelve. After she had successfully completed her GCSE's my good friend, Paul Heffer, suggested that Victoria (or Vix as she was now called) might like to go and spend a week at a Bible College in Saltcoats, near Glasgow, run by a group called the "Come back to God Campaign".

To our surprise Vix agreed to go, "just for a week", but she wanted to come home on the Saturday as she didn't want to have to go to church at the college on the Sunday. On the Friday Vix called to ask if she could stay another week – even though she would need to attend church. Of course, we agreed, and very surprisingly the following Friday she phoned again and asked the same question! On the third week she called and told us she'd given her heart to Jesus. Praise the Lord!

After spending nearly a year at the college she returned home and subsequently gained a degree in youth work and ministry with the Oasis Trust – she had always been good with children, and particularly with troubled kids. Eventually Vix travelled to the US for a year and stayed with our friends in Wyoming, working as an intern with the church and helping in youth camps. Since then, she has spent most of her working life helping young people in one form or another.

When we married, Wendy completed her nursing training at Addenbrookes Hospital in Cambridge, and after that we had a conversation about whether we would have a child together. We wondered whether we should, and by way of confirmation a number of prophetic words followed – but I'll save that story for a later chapter.

13. Egypt

A chance meeting

When Wendy and I married and moved into our current home, I didn't know anyone in the area. Wendy had a network of friends and colleagues because she was already working as a community nurse in a local doctor's practice. We began to pray that I would make some good, close local friends.

Each Christmas the doctor's practice would organise a dinner to which they invited everyone who worked there and their spouses. That year it was held later, on Burns night, and I went along not knowing anyone. Guests were deliberately placed with people they didn't know to (hopefully) encourage conversation, and you changed places with every course.

During the first course I overheard one of the GPs mention that she and her husband drove into London every Sunday to attend church. I wasn't part of the conversation, but made a mental note to ask her about it later. I didn't recall Wendy saying that she worked with any Christians.

Later, I managed to chat to this lady, Clare, and discovered they went to Holy Trinity Brompton. She introduced me to her husband. John O'Dowd is an internationally renowned spinal surgeon, whose client list includes members of the Royal family – not that he'd tell you that. We immediately hit it off and I knew there and then that John would become one of the close friends I'd been praying for.

In time, the friendship extended to our children too, as John's eldest daughter, Iona, was at school with my son, Seth, when he joined Monkton Combe School for the Sixth Form. Incidentally, Monkton, an amazing Christian boarding school near Bath, was one of the best things that ever happened to Seth, as it not only gave him a superb education at A level, but also shaped his character in a very special way. I'm also privileged to be godfather to John and Clare's youngest daughter, Isla.

A year after we first met, John suggested I meet someone he knew. It was through this meeting that I met another doctor who is now a dear friend and my GP, Peter Bibawy. I find it fascinating how God creates seemingly random connections that turn out to be strategic. Again, the friendship extends to our families. Peter's son, Philip, became best friends at school with Seth when he was at Salesian College in Farnborough.

Peter is Egyptian, and it was through him that I first heard in depth about what was going on in Egypt, and indeed he sparked my great interest in the nation.

Peter's background and upbringing was rooted in Coptic Orthodox Christianity, but Dalia, his wife, was an Evangelical. He shared with me his passion to see Egyptians come into a deeper relationship with Jesus Christ. He explained to me his vision to hold a prayer meeting for Egypt in London and invite as many of the Egyptian Diaspora as possible to attend.

I told him that CSW organised many similar country-focused prayer meetings, and that we could help organise such a day, perhaps even making Egypt CSW's special focus for the year ahead.

The team at CSW agreed that 2011 should indeed include a strong focus on Egypt, and together with Peter, we set a date of 29 January 2011 for the prayer event.

That timing proved to be prophetic. On January 25, unprecedented protests broke out in cities across Egypt. On the eve of the prayer meeting, later designated, "The Friday of Anger", the protests intensified, as did the Government's response. That evening Peter invited a group of people, including my very dear friend Archbishop

Angaelos, the first Coptic Orthodox Archbishop of London, to supper at his home. We spent the evening glued to the television as news poured in about the revolutionary events happening in Tahrir Square in Cairo. That night President Hosni Mubarak appeared on state television to announce the dismissal of his cabinet.

It was clear that Egypt was facing a season of deep uncertainty, and that the prayer event wasn't just timely – it was essential.

Thirteen days after the prayer day President Mubarak fled to his residence in Sharm al Sheikh and stepped down.

The day itself was an incredibly strategic time, and I knew then that it would be important for CSW to visit the nation as soon as possible.

Trip to Egypt

Egypt was still in turmoil when I first visited. During the 'Revolution' Cairo had been described as a war zone after the initially peaceful but passionate protest escalated into a series of violent clashes.

One of the first people I met in Cairo was Pastor Sameh Maurice. Sameh leads Kasr El Dobara Evangelical church – a very large church situated right on the edge of Tahrir Square. The square, also known as "Martyr Square", is in the heart of downtown Cairo and had been the epicentre of the demonstrations. Sameh and his team set up a 'field hospital' on the church's grounds, took in those who were injured and cared for them. The church literally has its own casualty department and many members of the congregation are doctors.

Sameh cares deeply about his nation and was incredibly insightful about how the political turmoil would play out. When we met, he made a number of predictions about what would happen politically in coming years and how it would affect the nation. In time everything happened exactly as he said.

One of the first places I visited after spending time with Sameh was Anafora. Founded by Bishop Thomas, Anafora is a retreat centre about an hour's drive into the desert outside Cairo. Each morning they hold a Coptic Orthodox mass and every evening there is a time of prayer and reflection with Bible readings in the languages of all those present. They also have an extensive library, gardens, a farm and lots of rooms for private prayer and meditation. Working with Bishop Thomas, it was arranged that CSW would run a training programme for people of all denominations to learn how to advocate effectively for freedom of religion or belief.

Meeting Pope Shenouda

One of the highlights of this first visit for me was meeting the leader of the Coptic Orthodox church, Pope Shenouda III. He died in 2012, aged 88, having held the office for exactly 40 years, 4 months and 4 days.

I went to meet the Pope in the company of Archbishop – then Bishop - Angaelos, who had travelled from his base in the UK to facilitate the meeting. With me was CSW's chairman, Bishop John Perry, Baroness Elizabeth Berridge, who chaired the All Parliamentary Group for Freedom of Religion or Belief, CSW's Team Leader for Africa and the Middle East, and several CSW supporters.

It began as a very formal meeting. The Pope, attended by two Bishops, (his secretaries), was already on his throne, and we walked into the room and were introduced to him one by one. Bishop Angaelos and I sat on either side of him, and the rest of the party sat around the room. But, this was different from many other meetings I'd experienced in that, as soon as I met this man, I knew and felt I was in the presence of a man of God. Pope Shenouda exuded the love and presence of God.

Notwithstanding his godly presence, Pope Shenouda's opening

statement rather grated on me! He wanted to educate us on the history of the Church in Egypt, and said,

"The Church in Egypt was born out of persecution…"

He continued,

"St Mark came to Alexandria to preach the Gospel of Christ. He was persecuted and dragged through the streets by his neck until he was dead. That was the real birth of the Church in Egypt. We were born into persecution and we have been persecuted ever since. We just accept this as our lot."

I felt compelled to challenge this fatalistic attitude.

"*You* might be prepared to accept that, Your Holiness, but I'm not prepared to accept it," I told him. "You may not be prepared to speak out, but we are. The Word of God says in Proverbs 31:8 that we are to speak up for those who cannot speak for themselves. Either you are unwilling or unable to speak up, but we will speak out against injustice."

The Pope took my remarks seriously and this sparked an intense conversation that lasted for the next two hours – and we were only supposed to have around 30 minutes with him. The Pope's two secretaries were obviously well aware of this, and their body language became very agitated, as if to say, "Just get on with it and get out of here!"

Pope Shenouda, however, seemed to love interacting with us.

This visit to Egypt was what we termed at CSW a "Vision Visit", which meant we took a few of our staunch supporters with us. One of those supporters was retired GP, George Sadler who had faithfully supported us for many years. George also happened to be one of the most politically incorrect people I knew. In retrospect, it may not have been the wisest decision to put him in front of the Pope!

George is old school, and had already gotten into trouble during this visit. When we visited the pyramids one day, he was upset by the overenthusiastic traders trying to sell their wares to tourists.

"Go away!" George would exclaim, "I don't like Arabs!"

We were constantly trying to keep him out of trouble. Given this track record, I allowed him to meet the Pope, but cautioned him first:

"Now George, it's very important that you understand: the only people who are allowed to speak to the Pope are me and Baroness Berridge."

"Oh, of course!" he replied.

Pope Shenouda clearly impressed George and at the time it had just been announced that Rowan Williams would be retiring the following year. Suddenly, in the middle of our conversation, George piped up from the back of the room:

"We're going to have a vacancy soon for the Archbishop of Canterbury. I really think you ought to apply, you'd do a far better job than the current guy!"

This was the only time in the meeting that the Pope was lost for words. Baroness Berridge stared at the ceiling, bit her lip and tried not to laugh, while I set about trying to rescue the situation.

As the meeting ended and we parted company, the Pope gave me a signed copy of a book as a gift. All of his sermons were transcribed and eventually published and this was a collection of some of his messages. It was a special gift and I was touched by this deeply spiritual man.

The Cave church

Later on in our visit, we had the opportunity to visit the Cave Church in the Muqattam– an amazing place with an incredible story. It is located in Manshiyat Nasser, a Cairo suburb otherwise known as Garbage City, which is inhabited by the *Zabbaleen* (literally "garbage people"). It is also a Christian district.

Around 15,000 tons of the Cairo's refuse is literally stacked around the base of the Muqattam Hills, due to the Cairo Metropolitan Area lack of a garbage collection system, despite having a population of 20 million. The Zabbaleen, predominantly Coptic Christians, run a door-to-door collection service for Cairo's residents and literally take the rubbish home with them, where they recycle it and either sell sorted garbage to middle men or use it to create something new.

The story of the Cave Church begins in AD 979. The Fatimid Caliph al-Mu'iz laid a challenge before the 62nd Pope of Alexandria. It was simple: the Christians faced being put to the sword unless the Pope could demonstrate that the Word of God was true, and that faith could indeed cause a mountain to move, as Matthew 17:20 declares.

The Pope called for three days of prayer and fasting and sought out the help of a Godly man, Simon the Tanner. After fasting, the Pope and Simon led a group of Christians to the foot of the Muqattam mountain. After conducting a mass, the Pope knelt and prayed for God's mercy in front of their oppressors. After prayer, an earthquake shook the mountain, which moved visibly several times.

After this the Caliph, convinced by the sign from God, allowed the Christians to build churches in the area including the Cave Church, in the very mountain that had moved.

Built inside a vast natural cave in the heart of the hills, the church is capable of seating up to 20,000 people. It has an average congregation of around 4,000 who meet in the lower sanctuary, but during the 2011 Revolution, an estimated 40,000 Christians gathered, overflowing into the grounds of the surrounding monastery, to pray for their nation.

President Sisi

My next visit to Egypt was in February 2014, following the removal six months earlier of President Morsi of the Muslim Brotherhood after huge nationwide protests. This time I was part of a Parliamentary delegation which, amongst others, included Baroness Berridge and Stephen Timms MP. My friend and doctor Peter Bibawy was also part of this visit.

On this occasion we met with many senior figures in the interim Government, as well as the Grand Imam of al-Azhar. However, the highlight of this trip was a meeting with the then Commander-in-Chief of the Armed Forces, and the main person behind the removal of President Morsi: Field Marshal Abdel Fatteh el-Sisi. At that moment in time Sisi was being encouraged to run for the Presidency, so he was considering retirement from the military in order to become an official candidate.

We were told that we'd get around 30 minutes with him, but rather like our meeting with Pope Shenouda, this one lasted nearly three hours.

Although an interpreter was present, initially Sisi spoke to us in English and told us that he had spent a very enjoyable year in Camberley (just a few miles from my home in Farnham) where he had undergone training at the Royal Military Academy, Sandhurst.

Nearly all of us found Sisi inspiring to listen to and there was a general feeling amongst us that this was a man to be taken very seriously.

Baroness Berridge and I put many questions to him concerning religious freedom and equality of citizenship in Egypt. He told us he believed in religious freedom too and acknowledged that Christians had always been treated as second class citizens in Egypt, but added that he didn't believe this should be the case.

He explained to us how, following the mass protests, he had challenged President Morsi three times to stand down, but he had refused. That's when the decision was made to seize control. Then he said that on his instructions the Grand Imam was informing the mosques what should be preached each week, to prevent the further spread of extremism and religious hatred. At one point I told him,

"I can see why you're doing that, but you need to be careful, because that's not necessarily a good thing for religious freedom. It could be a slippery slope and may lead to dictating what can and cannot be preached in churches too."

At this, his friendly demeanour dropped and he began to get animated.

"You don't understand what we face in this country!" he said in a raised voice.

Eventually, he calmed down and explained that he was determined to deal with Islamic extremism, but he was in a very difficult situation. Throughout the meeting both Peter and I prayed silently for this man, who we knew was almost certain to become the next President of the nation. He was already considered a great hero by many Egyptians for having gotten rid of Morsi.

At the end of our meeting, Sisi insisted on escorting us out of the building and I found myself walking beside him. As we walked down the staircase, I put my arm around him and said,

"Field Marshall, I want you to know that if you become President of this nation I will pray for you every day."

He stopped and looked at me.

"Do you mean that?" he asked.

"Of course," I replied.

"Honestly," he told me, "I don't want to be President of this country. It is an inferno. I don't desire to be President, but if the people want me to do it, then I will. But I can't do it without God's help. So I need you to pray for me."

"I will," I promised.

By this time the rest of our party were inside the waiting cars. Sisi walked me down to my car and as I got in, said,

"You won't forget that promise you just made me, will you?"

"No, I won't."

Within four months he was elected President, and was sworn in on 8 June 2014.

* * *

I met him again, as part of another, slightly larger parliamentary visit, just a few weeks after he had become President. In the meantime an Egypt All-Party Parliamentary Group (APPG) had been set up in Westminster, and members on this particular visit included four very good friends of mine, John Glen MP, Jeffrey Donaldson MP, Jim Shannon MP and my old travelling companion from the Russian visit, Sir David Amess MP. At first we were told it might be very difficult to get to see the president on this occasion, but they managed to find a time in his schedule. Then we were told by his officials that only members of the British Parliament could meet him, but one of the MPs asked the officials to pass on the message that I was with the party and had a good relationship with the President. I wasn't sure he'd remember my name, but he said yes, I could see him.

We met with Sisi for about an hour and, as we left, we all filed past him to shake his hand. When I shook hands with him he said,

"The last time you were here you made me a promise. Have you kept it?"

"Yes," I said, "I pray for you every day."

"Thank you so much," he said.

President Sisi is trying to be true to his word to bring equality to his great nation, but it's a difficult task. He's the only President to ever attend mass at St Marks Coptic Orthodox Cathedral during Christmas and New Year, and has made an effort to build a strong relationship with the Pope. He has also rebuilt some of the churches that were destroyed by the Muslim Brotherhood, and called for three days of national mourning when a group of Coptic Christians were beheaded in Libya.

I have a real heart for the Egyptian people, and President Sisi in particular. No leader can get everything right and he has made errors, some of them severe, but I do believe he's trying to do what's best for his nation. Sadly, there are still problems for Christians and other religious minorities in the nation, and you can be sure we will continue speaking out against all injustices, but we'll also be praying for President Sisi to succeed in building a just, prosperous, and secure nation, with full equality of citizenship.

14. China

In 2001, Lizzie, one of our advocates, arranged for us to take a trip to China. Accompanying Lizzie and I were David Shearman and Jonathan Aitken. The purpose of the trip was to visit various locations in China and Laos. The trip would then conclude in a third nation where, at a secret location, we would meet with some North Korean defectors.

Although I didn't know him personally at this point, I was aware of David Shearman by reputation. He led the thriving Christian Centre in Nottingham, where my sister Meg and her husband, David, were members. For a while I'd thought that David Shearman would be a great person to have on our board. However, Meg had told me more than once,

"David doesn't join boards."

Whenever I visited Meg, I usually went along to her church service and David was always gracious enough to greet me from the platform and speak in glowing terms of CSW.

Everyone I spoke to about it said that David would be a brilliant person to have on my board. But they also reiterated Meg's sentiments:

"David doesn't join boards!"

Instead of asking him outright, the next time I saw David I said to him,

"We're organising a trip to China in the next few months. Would you like to come?"

As a carrot, I mentioned that Jonathan Aitken was coming with us, who at the time was still very much in the news. I also thought that it would be good for Jonathan to meet David, as a hugely well-respected national Christian leader.

David agreed to come, and we all travelled out together on New Year's Eve, flying from London to Beijing.

We wanted to find out what conditions were like for Christians living in China, but I soon discovered that because China is so vast, conditions varied hugely from region to region. All the Christian commentators on China said the same thing. For this reason, we could never take a broad brush approach when speaking about the state of religious freedom in the nation.

It must be said that, at the time of our visit in 2001, things were beginning to improve slightly for Christians and for religious freedom generally. At the time of writing, however, sad to say the situation in China has degenerated into the worst since the end of the Cultural Revolution.

One meeting on our trip stands out in my mind. It happened at night when the four of us – me, Lizzie, David and Jonathan – were taken separately, and by deliberately circuitous routes, to visit the secret meeting of an underground church taking place in an apartment block.

We rendezvoused outside the apartment and our guide gave a special knock on the door. The door opened and the room was packed full of young students from the university, all sitting on the floor with Bibles, listening intently to a pastor who was teaching them from the Scriptures. At one point, David turned to me and said,

"This is our family."

It was such a poignant moment; it perfectly summed up how we all felt. This was indeed our family, and seeing all these young people hungry for the Word of God was so moving – especially in a country where they could all have been in great trouble for meeting together.

On the way back to our hotel that evening, Jonathan Aitken was feeling sorry for me because, due to my usual fussy eating habits, I had so far virtually starved on the trip. At one point we found ourselves passing a McDonalds, and Jonathan insisted we stop while he went in to buy me a Big Mac and fries. Jonathan was in there for ages and from our mini-bus we could see him desperately trying to make himself understood to the Chinese employees. Eventually, he emerged triumphantly with a huge bag in his hands and passed me my supper. I'm not sure about Jonathan's Mandarin, but inside the bag I found my Big Mac surrounded by twelve bags of fries!

During our stay in China we met many passionate-but-secret believers. In Guangzhou we visited the well-known underground church leader Pastor Samuel Lamb. We met him in his house, or should I say houses! He had bought several properties next to each other, which from the outside looked like a normal row of houses, but inside the adjoining walls had ingeniously been removed to accommodate his House Church.

Pastor Lamb had spent over twenty years in prison for his faith, and his hands and body carried the scars of heavy labour in the camps where he had been incarcerated. He was an elderly man and had a sparkle in his eye as he told us that despite constant threats to close down his church, he now had around five thousand believers regularly meeting together in his very specially adapted home. We came away laden with many theological books which he had written and printed on his secret press. What an inspiration!

Next, we travelled to Laos – the only landlocked country in Southeast Asia, bordered by China, Myanmar, Vietnam, Cambodia and Thailand. We visited a church in the capital, Vientiane, and spoke to its leaders. This particular church was thriving. They had around 300 members and had recently baptised many new Christians. It was a real oasis in the city.

We discovered, however, that out in the countryside, in remote villages, Christians were being persecuted very badly. The government was trying to force Christian pastors to sign agreements promising they would not sing hymns with the name of Jesus in them; that they wouldn't read the Bible or preach the Gospel – and a whole list of other things designed to close down their faith.

We were introduced to a young girl who told us her story. She said that her father, who was a widower, looking after five children, was one of the pastors who had refused to sign up to the government's demands.

One day, as he was travelling home on his motorbike, a car with blacked-out windows pulled up alongside him. The rear window came down and a gunman shot at the pastor multiple times.

At that moment an extraordinary miracle took place: the bullets literally bounced off the pastor. He was wearing just a thin linen shirt and trousers, but none of the bullets pierced his skin and he came away from the incident completely unscathed.

The pastor refused to be silenced and continued preaching the Gospel as he had done before. A few months later, however, his house was raided and this time the secret police were successful in killing him, as well as murdering one of his daughters.

This is another mystery that only God knows the answer to: why this man was spared on one occasion and not another. It's impossible for us to understand why.

And here, now, was one of the surviving daughters of this faithful pastor, standing in front of us. I said to her,

"Please tell us, is there anything at all that we can do for you?"

"Yes," she said. "Please pray that the men who did this will find Jesus."

This statement, though utterly staggering to our minds, summed up the heart of the Christians who made up the persecuted Church in that nation.

* * *

Next, we travelled out of Laos to our final destination – an undisclosed location, where we met in secret with a number of defectors who had managed to escape from North Korea. They were, in fact, heading to South Korea, but had to do so travelling by a convoluted route – a journey that often took up to a year to make.

We met a young man, just twenty-one years old, who had been travelling for 18 months to escape North Korea – passing through many different locations.

He told us that both his parents were Christians. His father had managed to get hold of a short-wave radio when he'd been working abroad in Russia, and smuggled it back with him. It was illegal even to possess a radio, let alone smuggle one. Through the radio they heard about Jesus and gave their lives to Him. At home, the family would have secret worship times, which they held on random days, so that no neighbours would notice anything unusual and suspect them of having "church" each Sunday.

One day, tragically, his father went to work as normal but was taken by the authorities and never seen again. Three days after this, his mother urged her son to escape the country.

The boy's mother took him down to a quiet part of the Tumen river where they would be safe, far enough away from the strong arc lights dotted along the bank. The Tumen is over 300 miles long and serves as part of the boundary between North Korea and China. His mother had an inner tube from a truck tire and made him get in the water, floating in the tube. She instructed him,

"Stay alive. Be great. Have ambition. And be a witness to the world of what is happening to us in North Korea."

He told us that he was terrified and that it took him over seven hours to float to China. But once in China he was able to rendezvous with some South Korean Christians and this was the beginning of his journey to freedom. Ever since, he was willing to tell his story to whoever he could, because that's what his mother had told him to do. The story of this remarkable, brave young man, was just one of so many similar accounts that we were beginning to hear.

Refugee Christians who are discovered in China are almost always sent back to North Korea, and if the authorities learn they have had any contact with Christians, they are likely to be executed. This is why it's so important for us to keep speaking out; to let the authorities know that the world is watching and is aware of the atrocious abuse of human rights.

* * *

David Shearman was hugely moved by this trip, seeing at first hand what life was like for many brothers and sisters in Christ in that part of the world. Thereafter, we would meet up whenever David was in London and, eventually, he did agree to join the board of CSW. David brought much worldly and spiritual wisdom and proved to be a fantastic addition to the board. He was an amazing supporter of CSW's work from 2003 until he retired in 2017, and remains a great friend and mentor to me personally.

15. Korea

If you look at night time satellite pictures of Korea, you can see that South Korea is alive with lights, while North Korea is mostly black with a few pinpoints of light, which highlights the austerity of the northern regime, but is also a metaphor for the nation's spirituality. In the south, a large percentage of the population are Christian. In the north there is virtually no church. The south sends out more missionaries to other parts of the world, per head of population, than any other nation on earth.

Although more recently North Korea has been in the news, for decades it has been shrouded in mystery and it has been hard to determine the state of wellbeing of Christians who live there.

Although as explained in the last chapter we had heard one or two first-hand accounts of persecution in North Korea, it was a couple of years later before CSW began to gather major evidence about major human rights abuses in that country.

Just before one of our annual conferences Lizzie approached me, feeling that the time was right to share some of this information. Our conferences always have a very tight schedule, with speakers coming from around the world, and last minute additions to the schedule can be very difficult to facilitate. To be fair, Lizzie had just returned from a trip where she had gathered many new, first-hand testimonies, but when she asked me for 10 or 15 minutes, I initially said no.

To her credit, she pestered me some more and told me just a couple of the stories that she'd heard. There were numerous Christians in prison camps and many had been executed in horrific ways. Witnesses had reported some people literally being run over by steam rollers. Others had boiling oil poured over them. As soon as I heard this, I found a way to make space in the schedule for her to speak.

Following on from this we decided Lizzie needed to produce a report of the state of religious freedom in North Korea. She subsequently authored an extensive and hugely important piece of work that became a catalyst for action. The report was called "North Korea: a Case to Answer, a Call to Act".

It was the first and most detailed report of its kind to be written and has been referred to many times since by all kinds of organisations set up in the wake of its findings. A great deal of sensitive information was collected, cross-referenced and corroborated by various North Korean defectors.

CSW has been one of the leading campaigning organisations for human rights in North Korea for many years now. One of the things we pressed for was a UN Commission of Inquiry into North Korea. Eventually, this did take place in March 2013, and we were asked to give evidence at it. The Inquiry was headed by an Australian former judge, Michael Kirby – previously a UN Special Representative on human rights in Cambodia. After the Inquiry he was reported widely in the press, saying that as a judge of 35 years, he had ruled on many harrowing cases, but had never encountered such atrocities before.

"There have been a number of testimonies which have moved me to tears," Kirby said, "and I am not ashamed to say that ... You would have be a stony-hearted person not to be moved by the stories that the Commission of Inquiry has received."

South Korea

Every trip I've taken over the years has been significant in its own way – either because I made an important new contact or was able to meet and hear the story of someone we were trying to help.

One time I visited Seoul and was accompanied by my friend Eddie Lyle who, at the time was CEO of Release International, and is now President of Open Doors UK. We travelled together to go to a conference and visit a number of churches, organised by our hosts, the Evangelical Alliance of South Korea.

Perhaps the most amazing part of this trip was visiting one of the many Prayer Mountains in and around Seoul. We drove up this particular mountain, facing North Korea and at the top discovered a large auditorium where prayer takes place continuously, day and night.

The main floor area was covered with sleeping bags, and it seemed that people went there to pray until they fell asleep. Around the mountainside were rows and rows of small booths. The idea is to kneel in a booth to pray for as long as you want. All around the mountain people were praying with great passion, wailing and crying out to God. The Koreans really know how to pray.

While I was in Seoul, I met a lady who had defected from North Korea. One morning over breakfast she told me her amazing story through an interpreter. I'll call her Annie.

Annie was a government official and had been travelling throughout North Korea on government business. At the end of her trip she was standing on the platform of a train station, waiting to catch her train home, when an old lady approached her.

The elderly woman started chatting to her and then began telling her about Jesus. By doing so she was, of course, risking her life. Mentioning the name of Jesus was outlawed in the nation, so anyone could report her to the authorities, but to make matters worse Annie worked for the government. It was Annie's duty to report this crime and turn the old lady in. The fate for anyone witnessing openly like this was immediate transportation to one of the notorious prison camps, but also quite probably execution.

However, Annie felt compelled to listen to what the woman was saying and, incredibly, she gave her life to Jesus right there, on the station platform. When Annie returned home, she kept her experience a secret. She was afraid to tell her husband what had happened and kept it a secret from her family.

Eventually, for a variety of reasons, Annie had escaped North Korea and recently defected to South Korea. It was here that someone had arranged for her to meet me at my hotel in Seoul. After she'd told me about how she came to Christ, she reached down and pulled two exercise books from her bag and showed them to me. They were both packed with handwritten notes and annotations in the margins, but all in Korean, so I couldn't understand a word.

"What are these books?" I asked. Through the interpreter she told me,

"These are the diaries of my spiritual journey."

I thought to myself, How can you have a spiritual journey when you can't even tell anyone you're a Christian?

The only Christian this woman had ever met, until now, was the old lady on the train station. She didn't belong to a church, she had no pastor, and she'd never had a Bible. I asked the interpreter to explain more and he began reading the pages of one of her journals. As he did so, his eyes filled with tears and, after reading for several minutes he said,

"This is amazing!"

He explained that Annie, who'd had no access to other Christians or any kind of Christian literature, had written down doctrine, verses of Scripture, and long personal reflections that spoke about the grace of God. It was utterly astounding.

As we talked it became clear to me that everything Annie had recorded in her journals she had received direct from the Holy Spirit. She had managed to grow and mature in her spiritual life without any of the things that Western Christians take for granted.

This encounter made me think when North Korea eventually opens up, there will be lots of people just like Annie – those who have come to faith in Christ and have been taught and nurtured by the Holy Spirit.

16. Seth

When we're young I guess that many of us just assume that one day, when we grow up, we'll get married and have children. For many people it happens, just like that, and for others it doesn't. Wendy and I were married and we were blessed to have Victoria, who was seven; we were happy. I didn't have any children of my own, but I treated Victoria like a daughter, and as far as I'm concerned she was, and still is my daughter.

Wendy and I discussed whether we'd try for a child together, but we'd just moved up to Cambridge and she was keen to complete her nursing training, so that decision was put on hold. In 1999, however, Wendy's sister had a baby and Wendy started getting a bit broody. By this time Wendy had finished her training and we agreed to pray to see if it was God's will for us to have a child.

However, time went on and we never really got around to praying about it, and one day while I was out driving I thought about this and wanted to bring it before God and square things off.

I had a long, very serious pray about the matter, then said to the Lord,

"God, if Wendy and I are to have any children of our own, you need to tell me today – and tell me in a way that I won't be able to mistake it's you speaking."

I was still working for *Sweet'n Low* at the time and was on my way to a sales call. To understand what happened next, I need to tell you that when I was a little boy I'd watched a cowboy film with a character in it called Seth. It may have been Seth Bullock, who was a real person – a contemporary of Wild Bill Hickok, and one of the best gunfighters in history. The name really appealed to me and it just stuck in my mind. From that moment on, I decided when I grew up and had a son, he would be called Seth. It was a fact that all my friends and family knew.

I walked into the foyer of the company I was visiting and spoke to a girl on reception about my appointment. While she was phoning the person I was due to see, I noticed a large clock on the wall behind her. On it was emblazoned the name "Seth Thomas". What I didn't know then, but realise now, was that Seth Thomas was a famous 19th century American clockmaker. However, most of the clocks bearing his name were antiques; it was extremely rare to see a more modern piece like this one with his name on it.

I was shocked that God chose to confirm that we would have a child in such a dramatic way. I was also delighted that God was showing me that we would have a son, being the last male of the Thomas family line. I decided to keep this information to myself and sit on it for the time being.

At the end of November 1999, I had just returned from a trip to Hong Kong and Wendy sat me down for a chat. We had not been trying for a child, but she said to me words to the effect of, "I don't quite know how this has happened… but, I'm pregnant!"

"Oh, that'll be Seth," I said without thinking.

"Oh, don't start," she said.

"Oh no, let me tell you the story," I said, and proceeded to explain what had happened.

After that, God was so gracious in giving us several more prophetic words confirming what would take place. In retrospect, I guess it might have been because at one point Wendy thought she was having an ectopic pregnancy and would lose the baby. God wanted to reassure us that this wouldn't be the case.

A week later a guest preacher visited our church and preached on the story of Elisha and the Shunammite woman. At one point he quoted the prophet,

"Next year at this time you will be holding a son in your arms!" (2 Kings 4:16 NLT)

The words jumped out at us and Wendy and I looked at each other. We knew that word was meant for us.

Around Christmastime we went to visit an old friend of ours in Grays, Joanne Godfrey. While we were sitting having a cup of tea, Jo said to Wendy,

"I'm not the kind of person who has dreams or visions, but I must tell you, the other night I had a very clear dream and in it, you and Merv were holding a baby boy."

Wendy and I looked at each other and both thought, "Wow!"

Then came a third confirmation. Normally I use *Every Day with Jesus*, but very occasionally I will read UCB's daily Bible reading notes in the morning. I decided to do that on the day we were due to have a scan at the hospital. The reading that day was from 1 Samuel 1:11, in which Hannah cries out to the Lord,

"Oh Lord … answer my prayer and give me a son, then I will give him back to you…"

We felt we'd received God's assurance that we would indeed have a boy.

At the hospital, the lady doing the scan asked us,

"Would you like to know the sex of the baby?"

"We already know," I replied.

"Well, you can't already know," she responded.

"Yeah, we do know," I said. "It's a boy."

"Right, OK," she said, perplexed, "well, it is in fact a boy."

The day that Wendy went into labour the midwife at the hospital asked her,

"Do you know whether you're expecting a boy or a girl?"

"Yes, a boy."

"Well, I need to tell you," she said, "we've had two in the last month who were expecting boys and they both turned out to be girls! So if that happens, don't be too surprised."

"No, no. This is a boy and his name is Seth," Wendy told her.

To her credit, the midwife took this on board and began saying, "Come on Seth!" as she encouraged Wendy to keep pushing.

The moment Seth was born, and I held him in my arms for the first time, I immediately prayed and "gave him back" to the Lord, committing him to God. It was a very precious moment.

The next thing I did, of course, was to put Arsenal booties on him! So he's never had any choice other than to be a Gooner.

* * *

Soon after Seth was born we decided to have him formally dedicated to God. Wendy and I wanted to make this a special event, rather than the usual five minutes in the middle of a regular Sunday morning service. We therefore chose a Saturday afternoon and invited all our oldest and best friends to our little Baptist church in Cambridgeshire. It was packed and was a wonderfully joyous occasion, led by our pastor Kevin Burdett. Our daughter, Victoria, read a beautiful poem and my brother-in-law, David Gill, preached a prophetic sermon over Seth.

We had thought very carefully and prayed about the important choice of godparents (or Spiritual Guardians as we called them). Apart from Jonathan Aitken and Paul and Norma Heffer (mentioned elsewhere in this book), we had asked our good friends David and Anita Bareham to perform this important task. For a number of years David had been

CSW's bookkeeper and together with Anita they later went on to plant a very successful Church in Chafford Hundred, near Grays.

One humorous incident happened during the service. When Kevin Burdett picked Seth up to pray his prayer of dedication, Seth decided to burp very loudly into Kevin's microphone. On the video of the afternoon, filmed by my old pal Stuart Windsor, at that point you can hear my friend Graham Bright saying in a loud stage whisper, "You can tell whose son he is!"

Afterwards, we held a reception in the village hall, during which I spoke, telling everyone of the prophecies God had given us about Seth's birth. Wendy and I then presented him with his own antique "Seth Thomas" clock, which still hangs in our hallway today.

To top off a very special afternoon, I can remember my cousin Mark, who as always on a Saturday afternoon, had his ear glued to a radio (well before the days of smartphones), suddenly announcing to all and sundry that Arsenal had just beaten Manchester City 5-0. What a glorious way to finish the day!

* * *

One night, when Seth was about five, he asked me,

"Dad, am I a Christian?"

"No," I told him. "Just because your mum and I are Christians doesn't make you one – you have to make your own decision." I was excited that he'd brought it up and asked him,

"Would you like to become a Christian then?"

"Well," he said in a considered manner. "That's the problem. Half of me wants to be a Christian and half of me wants to be naughty."

"That's true for all of us mate!" I told him, and explained in simple terms that the apostle Paul said exactly that in his teaching. Then I said,

"Well, when you're ready, let me know."

Each night, while he was asleep, I would go into his room and pray for him, as had been my habit with Victoria. When he was younger, he was playing football for Aldershot Town juniors and was a great little player. The club had a good chaplain, Mike Pusey and they used to have an annual carol service. One year when Seth was about seven, and we were driving home from the carol service, he asked me the same question.

"Dad, am I a Christian? Wasn't I born a Christian?"

I explained the situation again and asked,

"Why - do you want to become a Christian?"

"Yes, I do," he said.

"That's great Seth," I said.

"What do I need to do?" he asked.

"When we get home you just need to pray a little prayer," I told him.

"No, let's do it now," he said. We were only about half a mile from home, but he insisted, so he prayed there and then in the car and Seth became a Christian on a roundabout on the A331. On the following Sunday he told our pastor, Rob Lewis, what he had done, and Rob got him to tell the whole church.

Years before this, God had made it clear he had his hand on Seth. We were visiting my sister and brother in law, Meg and David, in Nottingham, and so attended their church, Christian Centre Nottingham for the Christmas service. My friend, David Hind, was leading the worship that morning. Seth had a terrible earache and I remember walking around carrying him, trying to console him. He was sobbing in pain and all I could think was, "Where on earth am I going to find some Calpol on Christmas Day?"

Just then David Hind came by and asked how I was and enquired after Seth. I told him Seth had really bad earache and David straight away laid his hand on Seth's ear and prayed,

"Lord, take this pain away."

Seth seemed to calm down. After the service, as we drove away, I said,

"OK, where can we find some Calpol for Seth?" But Seth piped up and asked,

"Daddy, why?"

"For your earache son," I replied.

"There's nothing wrong with it," he said. "Jesus took the pain away the minute that man touched my ear."

So Seth knew that God was real from a very young age.

Another amazing incident confirmed it for him when he was about 12.

Seth had been saving up for a FIFA football computer game and needed £48. He'd been putting away a couple of pounds here and there for quite a while and one day asked if we could count it together. It amounted to £58, so I said,

"There you go, you've got enough for your game."

Now Seth absolutely loved his football, and he really wanted this game, but he must have heard me talking about the work of CSW on many occasions and, after thinking for a minute, he said to me,

"Dad, I think my persecuted family needs this money more than I need a video game."

Although this was incredibly touching and wonderful, part of me thought, "The last thing I want to do is raid my 12-year old son's money box to fund the ministry. That doesn't seem right!" So I said to him,

“Listen, why don’t you go away and pray about it for a bit and see what God says? Don’t make an impulse decision.”

“Alright Dad, I will,” he said.

The next day he came back to me and said,

“I still want to give that money Dad.”

“You’ve got £58,” I told him. You could give £10 to CSW and still get your game.” But he said,

“No, I’ll give them £50 and I’ll keep £8.”

“You’re quite sure? You won’t get your video game.”

“That’s not important,” he said.

So together we sat on his bedroom floor and carefully counted out £50 in £1 and £2 coins and put it in a bag. I took the bag into the office the next day and put it on my desk. I used to go into work early at the time, often around 6.00 or 7.00am, while the office was quiet. Later, when I knew our finance director would be in, I thought I would take the money down to him. Before doing so, I emptied all the coins out and counted them one more time to double check. There was £50.

I went into Sina’s office and told him the story about Seth giving up his game in order to give CSW a gift for his persecuted family around the world. Sina became very animated at this and began praying out loud that God would bless Seth with a double portion for his faithfulness.

I returned to my desk, but a couple of hours later Sina phoned me from his office.

“Merv, how much did you say Seth wanted to give to CSW?”

“There’s £50 there, and he wants to give all of it,” I confirmed.

“OK then, so I’ll give you the other £50 back shall I?”

"What do you mean?" I asked, puzzled.

"Well, there is £100 in this bag," he explained.

"No, there's £50," I insisted. "I've counted it myself – twice!"

"There is definitely £100 in coins in this bag Merv," he told me.

Later Sina returned £50 to me and Seth got his computer game after all. Don't ask me how it happened – all I know is that God honours faith and sacrifice, and sometimes does so in amazing ways. I did explain to Seth that it wouldn't always happen that way!

17. Jonathan

At CSW we are very privileged to have the former Cabinet minister Jonathan Aitken as our honorary President. Jonathan has been a great friend and a key influence in my life for almost 25 years.

Sometime around 1994 my friend Paul Negrut from Romania wrote, asking me to get in touch with Jonathan to invite him to speak at the opening of their new church. I phoned Paul and queried this with him.

"Why do you want him? He's not really known as a Christian MP."

"Yes, he is," Paul said.

"I'm sure he's not," I told him.

"He is. He spoke at last year's Romanian Evangelical Alliance conference," he told me.

"Are you sure?" I said.

"Please just ask him," Paul implored me.

"OK, I'll write to him, but I'm pretty sure he won't come."

At the time, Jonathan was Defence Minister. I wrote to him, introducing myself, and mentioning that Paul Negrut wanted to invite him to Romania.

I didn't hear back, so I wrote again a couple of months before the church was due to open. I didn't get a response and I pretty much forgot all about it until one day I received a handwritten letter from Jonathan. In it he said he'd put my letter to one side in order to reply to it personally, then mislaid it. He apologised for not being able to attend the church opening and said he recalled speaking at the earlier conference, mentioning what a moving time that had been.

I thought it was decent of him to respond, so I wrote back to him thanking him for his letter and told him a little about the opening of the church. This was the beginning of a sporadic correspondence back and forth between us.

Later, when Jonathan was in the news, I dropped him a line from time to time to say that I was thinking about him and praying for him. He always wrote back and thanked me, saying that he really appreciated my prayers. After that, he began sending me Christmas cards. Though at this point we hadn't met, we sort of became pen friends.

It was in the April of 1995 that *The Guardian* newspaper published a front page report about Jonathan's dealings with leading Saudis and cast doubt on whether a stay in a Paris hotel had been paid for by an arms dealer. So began a well-documented court case that would dominate his life for the next four years.

We continued to write back and forth and I shared my faith with Jonathan. In one letter, just after his libel court case had collapsed in the summer of 1997, he wrote to tell me he'd received a letter from Chuck Colson and said, "He seems to be saying the same things as you about repentance and forgiveness." Colson happened to have been in London around the time that the news was filled with Jonathan's case, so he wrote him a letter of support, reflecting on his own well-documented troubles around Watergate and President Richard Nixon.

At that time I was living in Cambridge, but travelling down to London once or twice a week, so I wrote to Jonathan offering to meet up and pray with him, to support him as he continued his legal battles. I didn't expect him to take me up on the offer, but on the August bank holiday of that year he phoned me out of the blue and said,

"I wondered if I could take you up on your offer to come and pray with me?"

I said yes immediately and arranged to go and see him a few days later. I was a bit nervous about visiting him, but at the same time felt that God had given me a few things to say. There were photographers lurking in the street as I approached his famous, 8 Lord North Street house and knocked on the door.

Answering the door Jonathan seemed surprised to see me and I picked up a slight hint that he'd forgotten I was coming. Or perhaps, "I wish I hadn't asked this guy to come. I'll give him a quick coffee then get rid of him!"

However, we spent the best part of three hours talking and Jonathan poured his heart out to me. At the end I said to him,

"Well, shall we pray?"

"Yes," he said. "Oh, do you mean out loud?"

I asked him if he wanted to pray and he said he did, after which I prayed a long prayer over him. Then I told him,

"Look, you know where I am. If you ever want me to come again, I'm happy to do so."

He immediately got out his diary.

"Can we put a date in for next week?"

So I began visiting him every week after that. I also found out that he was being supported by a group of Christian MPs, including Alistair Burt, the late Michael Alison and former MP Tom Benyon. I would visit Jonathan on Tuesdays and this small group would pray with him on Thursdays.

Jonathan used to call me his spiritual tutor, and although I was far from qualified for such a title, we did begin working through Bob Gordon's book *The Foundations of Christian Living*, which was Bob's basic discipleship course.

On the eve of one of my weekly visits I was reading my Bible (Contemporary English Version) and the verse Matthew 5:25 leapt off the page:

"Before you are dragged into court, make friends with the person who has accused you of doing wrong. If you don't, you will be handed over to the judge and then to the officer who will put you in jail."

I thought, "This is for Jonathan", so I wrote it down, slipped it in my pocket and prayed for the Lord to give me the right opportunity to share it.

The next morning I sat there listening to Jonathan bitterly complaining about the Editor of the Guardian, Alan Rushbridger, blaming him for suggesting in a letter to the Director of Public Prosecutions that his wife, Lolicia, and daughter Victoria had conspired with him to pervert the course of justice.

I gently pointed out that it had been Jonathan's lies which had been at the bottom of it all, so he should blame himself, not the Editor of the Guardian. He accepted that, but told me that he had forgiven him anyhow! I wasn't so sure, so I pushed Jonathan on the issue and then quoted him Matthew 5:25.

After a little discussion, I suggested we might actually pray a prayer of forgiveness for Alan Rushbridger and the other Guardian journalists. I remember we had a wonderful time of prayer that morning. I knew it had made an impact on Jonathan when he told me he'd continued to pray those same prayers of forgiveness in his own private devotions in the days and weeks ahead. When we had finished praying Jonathan said he felt a real load had been lifted, and we laughed together as we wondered what the recipients of our prayers would have thought if they could have been a fly on the wall in Lord North Street.

Jonathan recounted this story in his book *Pride and Perjury* (Harper Collins), and when the book came out the Guardian carried a review, written by Alan Rushbridger himself. In the review he mockingly referred to, "Aitken going down on his knees with the improbable figure of the Sales and Marketing Director of Sweet'n'Low to pray for his soul"!

It was a few weeks after this that Jonathan told me he'd received a letter from an old school friend. The school friend was Sandy Millar, then vicar of Holy Trinity Brompton.

"He's suggesting that I go on something called the Alpha Course," Jonathan said. "What do you think?"

"If you go and take the Alpha Course you'll be in the newspapers the next day," I told him, "so you need to be ready for that. But, yes, you should do it."

Jonathan went and it did make the newspapers the very next day. The headline in the Daily Mail read, "Good God, now look who's here". Of course, it didn't deter Jonathan and he went on to complete the Alpha course, including the Holy Spirit weekend. He invited me along as his guest at the final Alpha Supper and we sat with Nicky Gumbel.

It was in June 1999 that Jonathan found himself in the dock at the Old Bailey, where he had pleaded guilty to charges of perjury. On the morning of the sentencing he had invited me to his home for a small breakfast with family and a few friends, including Chuck and Patti Colson, who had flown over from the USA especially. We all knew Jonathan would be sent to prison, but had a beautiful time of prayer with him, before we all trotted off to the Old Bailey. In some respects, I suppose it was a bit like being at the Last Supper!

Jonathan was sentenced to 18 months and taken off to the notorious Belmarsh prison. We corresponded while he was in prison and I tried to visit, but all kinds of obstacles were put in my way by the prison authorities, so I never actually got to see him.

Jonathan was released on licence after seven months, but just before his release he was allowed a visit home for Christmas – which the newspapers got steamed up about and called disgraceful. I phoned him on the Boxing Day and had a joyful conversation, anticipating the close resumption of our prayer partnership. It was during that call that

Jonathan became one of the first people to learn Wendy and I were expecting a baby. Subsequently, he would become Seth's godfather – a responsibility he has always taken very seriously, and they have a great relationship.

During Seth's final year at Barfield Prep school in Farnham, as Chairman of Governors I invited Jonathan to be guest of honour at speech day. When we announced it, the reaction was such that one would have thought we had invited a serial killer to speak! I had numerous emails from parents, telling me in no uncertain terms that it was a disgrace to invite such a man to address their children. There was quite an uproar – so much so that even the Head tried to persuade me to withdraw the invitation. Of course, I refused, and after speech day I was thrilled that many of those same parents wrote to say how wrong they'd been, and that Jonathan's quiet humility had been an inspiration to parents, teachers and children alike.

As our friendship continued, it seemed natural for me to invite him to become the CSW's Honorary President, and we subsequently travelled together on a number of trips for CSW, including to China. As busy as he is, he has always responded to whatever I've asked him to do.

Since Jonathan's release he has also been heavily involved in prison ministry and in July 2018 was ordained as a Deacon in the Church of England by the Bishop of London in St Paul's Cathedral.

Our friendship is stronger than ever and we still meet every few weeks to pray and share together. Without wanting to embarrass him, he has been a huge positive influence on my life for the last 25 years, in more ways than he'll ever know. I'm grateful for our friendship.

18. Nigeria

On my first visit to Nigeria I travelled with Dr Khataza Gondwe, an amazing advocate and CSW's Head of Advocacy. Also accompanying us was our finance director, Adesina (Sina) Adesanya.

From the airport we were driven to the city of Jos, in central Nigeria, to stay at the home of Bishop Benjamin Kwashi (now the Anglican Archbishop of Jos Diocese). Nigeria is a nation of two halves: the south is predominantly Christian with a smattering of Muslims, and the north is predominantly Muslim with a smattering of Christians. Jos is located right in central Nigeria, where the number of Christians is significant.

Archbishop Ben and I had previously met in London and he had spoken at one of CSW's conferences, so he had invited us to stay with him before we travelled up-country into the dangerous north.

Ben Kwashi and his lovely wife Gloria are a devout, gifted and formidable couple. Ben has never been afraid to speak out against injustice, and because of this, extremists tried to kill him on two occasions.

On the first occasion, Archbishop Ben was out of town. A group of men managed to gain access to their compound and smashed in the front door of his house at 2.00am. Upon finding he wasn't in the house, the men beat Gloria severely, temporarily blinding her in one eye, and told her they were going to kill her, but eventually left her alive.

After the first failed attempt, a year later a gang of around six men jumped the security guards at the gates of the family's compound, tying them up. Armed with guns and machetes they captured and locked up four domestic staff in the Archbishop's house, then smashed down his bedroom door.

Archbishop Benjamin was overpowered and dragged outside. The men were ready to murder him when he dropped to his knees and said,

"Before I die, I want to pray."

He closed his eyes, prayed silently and waited for the inevitable, but as he was praying the men inexplicably left. He later said,

"I have seen a miracle. Join me in thanking God that my life has been spared again."

* * *

You'll understand then, why I felt a bit nervous about staying in the Archbishop's home. We were only going to be staying there for one night, but my mind played tricks on me and I thought, "Tonight could be the night when the extremists come back!" I guess I'm a bit of a wimp really!

I was sharing a room with Sina, and we'd not long turned out the lights to go to sleep when I heard a loud noise outside our window that I was convinced was a lion.

Sina got up and looked out of the window to see what was going on, then began laughing. A cow had somehow gotten into the courtyard below our window and was mooing very loudly!

Then, in the morning, I awoke to a loud voice outside chanting in Arabic.

"Oh no," I thought. "This really is it!"

Again, Sina had to reassure me it was not an attack – it was the daily call to prayer from a nearby mosque.

The next morning we rose early to leave Jos and travel north. We were travelling in the car of the head of an NGO we were partnering with at the time, who was taking us to Maiduguri in the far northeast of the country to visit victims of the 2006 Danish Cartoon Riots. Maiduguri is the capital and largest city of Borno State, founded in 1907 as a British military outpost, and the HQ of the terrorist group Boko Haram.

Before we left, Gloria Kwashi informed us there had been tension in Jos in the days preceding our arrival. As we drove through the city, it was eerily quiet. We later found out that a few minutes into our journey, she had received information about some trouble taking place along the route we were to travel. She wanted to advise us to go via a different road and avoid the main route, because a large group of people were rampaging on the streets of Jos and causing all sorts of problems. However, she could not get through because the phone network had been brought down, possibly by the Plateau State authorities to thwart any attempts to organise a riot.

* * *

In February 2006 Maiduguri was the scene of infamous riots sparked by the publication of cartoons depicting the Prophet Mohammed in Denmark in which 57 churches were destroyed and over 60 Christians were killed.

It was a dangerous place for us to visit, but we wanted to meet with some of the Christians there to hear their stories and offer our prayers, support and encouragement. The stories of those we met were in stark contrast to each other.

We first met a couple, Joseph and Hannatu. They had three children and belonged to a local church. On the day of the Cartoon Riots, Hannatu had gone to a church prayer meeting, leaving Joseph at home with five children – their own three, plus their niece and nephew who were staying with them – all under the age of 12.

Sometime later Joseph heard a commotion down the street and looked outside to see what was happening. The family lived in a Christian enclave, and a neighbour alerted Joseph that an extremist mob was coming down their street, forcing entry into every home and burning it down.

On the spur of the moment, Joseph told us, he made a terrible decision that he would regret for the rest of his life. Because the mob were breaking into homes and setting fire to them, he told the children to flee through the gate while he clambered over a tall wall at the back of the house.

"They won't touch young children," he thought. "They are just after the adults."

The five children either returned to the house in fear or were pushed back into the house by the extremists, who set it on fire.

Joseph reconnected with Hannatu and they later returned to the house, desperately looking for the children. In the wreckage of their still smouldering home they found the charred bodies of all five children in the living room. They were in a circle, all holding hands. Clearly, they had come together and prayed in the same way they did each day at morning devotions.

Joseph and Hannatu had been rehoused by the time we met. Hannatu told us that for a while she had been particularly tormented about the agony the children must have experienced before dying. One night, soon after this terrible incident, God gave her a dream in which the children came to her and said,

"Don't worry, as soon as we held hands, heaven opened and Jesus took us to be with Him."

In a different part of Maiduguri, we met Pastor Augustine and his wife Ruth who told us a very different story, having lived through the same turmoil.

Augustine was at home with the children when the riot started. He had a dilemma: he was the pastor of a local church. Should he flee for his own safety, or should he stay for the sake of his church? He had no idea what to do for the best, but in the end decided to sit tight and prayed, "Lord, I'm staying. You've got to protect me!"

Eventually, a gang of armed men arrived at his house and began breaking down the gate. He heard many raised voices. They were shouting,

"A pastor lives here who teaches people the Bible. His wife is also a pastor. Let's bring them outside and kill them."

Augustine stretched his hand towards the gate and commanded it not to yield.

He returned to the house, hid his wife and children in the farthest recesses of the house, and sat in front of their hiding place.

The men broke down his door and rushed into the place where he was sitting in prayer. He closed his eyes, remained sitting on his chair, and prayed silently, asking God to help him. He heard the sound of people moving around him and heard their conversation.

"There is nobody here. Go upstairs and check all the bedrooms."

More noise of people moving around upstairs, then the sound of them returning to the living room.

"It's empty, I can't find anyone."

"OK, let's move on."

Then silence.

Augustine opened his eyes and he was alone. God had performed a miracle and hidden him from their sight.

This first gang left him alone and contented themselves with looting the house, taking everything of value.

Later a second armed gang came and actually cornered Augustine. One of them raised his dagger over his head to deliver a fatal blow, but his arm became paralysed and he couldn't strike Augustine. A look of shock spread across the man's face. Gradually, they all backed away and left Augustine standing alone.

However, his ordeal was not yet over - yet another gang of armed men appeared and surrounded him.

"Surely this is it," he thought. "I can't survive a third attack."

However, just as he thought the end had come, a large Muslim man who was part of the crowd ran forward, stood in front of him and said:

"If you want to kill this pastor, you've will have to kill me first."

The group left, and when Augustine went to thank the man, he was nowhere to be seen!

I'm at a loss to explain the stark difference between these two stories. Five children were burnt to death, but a pastor and his children were spared. All I know is that in the roll call of faith we read in Hebrews 11, some people escaped being eaten by lions, burned alive, or being put to the sword, while others, it says, were stoned, "sawn in half" or killed with the sword. All were commended for their faith. We can't guess at the reasons why God allowed one circumstance or the other. All I know is that I considered all the believers we met in Maiduguri to be heroes of the faith. They all had an amazing resilience in their commitment to Christ.

* * *

As we drove north it soon became apparent that our Nigerian colleague had a unique manner of driving, and I began to feel pretty uncomfortable.

We were travelling in a 4x4 jeep and he seemed determined to maintain speeds of up to 100 miles per hour, even along poor roads that were littered with potholes. Not only that, but at times he was texting on his mobile. Khataza was sitting upfront, next to him, and Sina and I were in the back along with one of his staff members. At one point he was still speeding along, driving one-handed whilst drinking a bottle of Coke, when he hit a pothole at 90 miles per hour.

The jeep veered left into the lane of oncoming traffic, then careered off the road into the bush and we were ploughing through scrubland, completely out of control. It happened very quickly, but there was still time for my life to flash before me. I honestly thought. "This is it, we're all going to die!" Suddenly the vehicle stopped abruptly. Gathering myself I saw that Khataza's face and clothing were covered with a dark substance. Initially, I thought it was blood, but it turned out to be the driver's Coke that had gone everywhere. A worship CD had been playing on the car stereo as we drove, and as we sat there in shock the singing continued, "Jesus saves, Jesus saves…"! No one was hurt and we were very grateful Jesus did in fact save us.

* * *

We visited a number of other places on our journey back from the north. We made a brief stop in a city called Gombe – the capital of Gombe State in the north east of the country. The most notable thing about this place for me, was the sense of spiritual oppression that hit you as you entered the city. It was almost tangible, as though a cloud hung over the place following the lynching by students and townsfolk of Christiana Oluwasesin, a married Christian school teacher and mother of two, who had been falsely accused of desecrating a Quran in March 2007.

We returned to Plateau State before travelling to the capital of Nigeria, Abuja, in the centre of the country. Here we were able to meet with some members of the Nigerian parliament. I spoke to them about what we had witnessed in the north, but was disappointed by their apathetic reaction.

After speaking with a group of parliamentarians Khataza, Sina and I were invited into the office of a lady MP, Beni Lar who represented Langtang North/South constituency in Plateau State. I was speaking about the UK and US prayer breakfasts that brought together Christians from all political persuasions. I told her how, in Westminster, I knew of a group of six MPs – Labour, Liberal Democrats and Ulster Unionists – all with very different views, who prayed together regularly despite their differences. As I spoke, it became obvious that Christians in the Nigerian Houses of Assembly had little to do with one another, let alone prayed together. This lady was interested to see if something similar could be set up in Nigeria.

The following year, Khataza returned to Nigeria with two British Christian MPs, Andy Reed and Gary Streeter, and David Smith, a representative from the UK Bible Society. This visit laid the foundation for a regular Nigerian parliamentary prayer breakfast that would bring together Christian MPs from across the nation. The year after that, I was privileged to be invited to their first ever prayer breakfast.

* * *

My most recent visit to Nigeria took place towards the end of 2017, and this time I took Seth along with me. He was 17 years old, and had always wanted to accompany me on one of my trips. However, I'm not sure Wendy was too keen that he should choose Northern Nigeria for his first mission!

After participating at a conference in Abuja, we were able to attend the Parliamentary Prayer Breakfast as the guests of Rev Yunusa Nmadu, General Secretary of one of Northern Nigeria's largest denominations, the Evangelical Church Winning All (ECWA). As we sat down, I felt very honoured to be approached by a parliamentarian who remembered the role I had played in starting this event, and who asked me to say a few words from the podium. What a privilege!

After leaving the Prayer Breakfast we started our journey northwards on the Abuja to Kaduna road, which at time of writing is still notorious for kidnappings. Our purpose was to visit one of the Christian villages that had been affected by attacks from armed Fulani Herdsmen, also known as the Fulani Militia.

The Fulani are a nomadic, predominantly Muslim, tribe that are found across West Africa. While many are peaceable herders, a sizeable number are part of a deadly militia operating in the north and centre of Nigeria that was named the fourth deadliest terrorist group in the world in 2013 by the Global Terrorism Index.

They have been targeting non-Muslim communities, particularly Christians, and Southern Kaduna (where we were travelling), happened to be one of the worst affected areas. At that time more than 800 men, women and children had already been killed and over 10,000 had fled their homes.

We hadn't gone very far when we were waylaid on the outskirts of Abuja by a criminal gang who tried to extort money from us, saying they were in charge of selling passes that allowed vehicles to use the road. Seth and I were travelling with Rev Yunusa Nmadu, who apart from his role with ECWA is also the CEO of CSW Nigeria. Yunusa was very angry and refused outright to pay this gang any money at all. The result was that one of them jumped into the back of our vehicle alongside Seth and me, and made us drive off the road to their "HQ" in a small, gated shopping area.

Apparently, while we had been refusing to pay and demanding to see their leader, they had set up a chair and desk in a small empty shop, where a man pretended he was their leader and proceeded to negotiate with members of CSW Nigeria, who were travelling in the car behind us with CSW UK staff. We were all praying we would be allowed to go without having to pay what was effectively a bribe, and after a delay of about 90 minutes our prayers were answered. We were on our way again.

After a couple of hours, and numerous legitimate army roadblocks later, at last we pulled off the main road. We then bumped our way along several miles of dirt roads until we reached our destination, Asso Village.

Twenty-two people had already been killed in Asso that year by the militia. The first attack happened on Easter Day, when the gunmen burst into their church killing a dozen worshippers.

We were taken into their village hall where around 60 or 70 villagers were gathered, and we listened to their stories. At one point they brought in a 15-year old boy on crutches. His name was Jude Bartholomew. We soon saw why he couldn't walk properly – his leg was hugely swollen with a gaping, open and infected wound.

A couple of months previously Jude was going to the market square when he heard the sound of gunfire. He was about to run when he felt his leg go numb. Looking down he saw blood flowing from his lower leg and knew he had been shot. He stumbled into a nearby field and lay there, pretending to be dead. The gunmen approached Jude, saw the blood, and decided he was dead. They then entered a nearby house and killed the man they found there before leaving.

Jude was taken to a hospital in a town several miles away later that night, where the bullet was removed. The family could not afford the on-going transportation and treatment costs, so were treating him with traditional herbal medicines. But Jude's leg was deteriorating, and one of the first things Yunusa did was to give instructions for him to be taken to a hospital in neighbouring Plateau state for treatment. I'm pleased to say Jude's leg was saved.

After listening to the village elders, I stood up to speak.

"If I could give you one thing, what would it be?"

Eventually, an older man stood up and said,

“We just want peace. We are for peace and even the Fulanis know it. We have lived with these people for years. They used to just carry sticks and now they have AK47’s.”

Another said,

“Please pray for us. They are in the fields all around our village, and we are frightened to go and farm our lands, which means we are beginning to starve.”

It was heart breaking and at times like these there is not much else you can do but turn to God in prayer. As I stood and prayed I could hear “amens” and “hallelujahs” echoing around the hall.

As we were standing talking before leaving the village, Seth came alongside me and said,

“Dad, it should be compulsory for all Western Christians to come to this village.”

“Why?” I asked.

“Because despite living in absolute fear, and gradually starving, it’s clear they have joy in their hearts – they have Jesus. Back home in our churches people moan and complain about every little thing.”

How right he was!

When we got into the car to leave Asso, I could tell something was greatly troubling Seth. As we drove out he asked Yunusa why the young boy, Jude, had not been able to get treatment for his badly infected leg. Yunusa explained that the nearest hospital was 25km away, and even if they had managed to get him there, the family would not have had the money for treatment.

What Seth said next shocked me.

"Why can't we build a hospital here in Asso? How much would it cost?"

Yunusa made a couple of phone calls and told him it would cost around £50,000 to build and equip, and if a hospital could be built, ECWA would take over and run it.

"OK, I'll raise the money," said Seth. "Can you get me an official estimate to build and equip a hospital/clinic please Yunusa?"

Well, I'm ashamed to say that Dad did his best to explain to his son that raising £50,000 wasn't that simple, and that he shouldn't make such rash promises.

However, I think that both Yunusa and I had a feeling that this boy was going to be as good as his word.

* * *

On returning home, the first thing Seth did was to email Chris Wheeler, his Headmaster at Monkton, and asked to see him first day back at school. Chris not only saw him, but believed in what Seth was trying to do. He agreed that, with his support, Seth could pitch for the hospital project to be the official Monkton Charity of the Year. Each year all the pupils get to vote for the charity they want to support, and it is to Seth's great credit that he made the case for Asso in such an inspirational way that he got 75% of all the votes!

Seth then set up a Just Giving page online and the first donation into that fund was £500 – all the money he had earned lifeguarding that summer. He was determined that if he was asking others for money, he was going to put his own money where his mouth was.

Early on I suggested he might approach my friend, Floyd Brobbel, at Voice of the Martyrs in Canada for a donation, as I knew they had done some work in Nigeria. About 30 minutes after he'd emailed Floyd, I had a very excited Seth on the phone to me.

"Dad, your friend has said that VOM Canada will match every pound I raise up to a maximum of £25,000. Hallelujah!"

To cut a long story short, nine months after our visit to Asso, £50k had been raised and the foundations were laid for their very own hospital. The villagers of Asso, I'm sure, are so glad that this young man didn't look at their hopeless situation and ask "Why?" Instead, he believed he could make a difference and asked, "Why not?"

19. Iraq

Towards the end of July 2016, I received a call from my old friend Frank Wolf. Frank had retired from Congress at the beginning of 2015 and, at the time of his announcement, was Virginia's longest standing congressman, having served for 34 consecutive years. He was now working with an organisation called 21st Century Wilberforce, based in Falls Church, just outside Washington D.C. – an advocacy and human rights organisation dedicated to empowering religious freedom for everyone, very similar to CSW.

21st Century Wilberforce had already had a conversation with our Middle East Advocate about a trip to Iraq and Kurdistan, and enquired whether I would be willing to visit there, but I wanted to hear from Frank himself about the aims of the trip.

If I'm honest, I wasn't bursting with enthusiasm to visit this part of the world, renowned as it is as a hotbed of religious and political turmoil, but Frank can be very persuasive.

"I'm going and I want you to come with me, Merv. We haven't been on a trip together for a few years and it'll be a great reunion."

I could think of better places to have a reunion, but replied,

"That's nice, but that can't be the purpose of the trip, Frank."

At the time my knowledge of this part of the Middle East was fairly limited. Our Middle East involvement up until then had mainly been in Iran, Egypt, Turkey and latterly Syria. Kurdistan, however, I knew virtually nothing about. Frank told me,

"The purpose will be to ascertain what the conditions are like there for Christians, and to find out what we in the West can do that would encourage Christians to continue living in the region."

You have to remember that many of the events in the Bible took place in modern day Iraq. The great patriarch Abraham came from Ur in southern Iraq, modern Nasiriyah, and Rebekah came from northwest Iraq. Additionally, Jacob's sons, the 12 tribes of Israel, were all born in Iraq and Daniel lived in Iraq most of his life.

In Mosul we found the tomb that is universally acknowledged by Christians, Muslims and Jews as the resting place of Seth, the third son of Adam and Eve, and brother to Cain and Abel. According to Genesis 4:25 Seth was born after Abel's murder.

Despite this, the Christian community in Iraq has been largely forgotten by many in the West. A decade ago there were some 2 million Christians living in Iraq. Today there are around 200,000. Were there things we could do to reverse the trend of Christians having to flee their homeland?

But I needed to be reassured that everywhere Frank and his colleagues went on this trip, I would be with them. Although Frank is a retired congressman, he is still considered a senior political figure around the world, and I had known trips where the organisers had told me, "Mr Wolf is going on this part of the trip, but you can't." As there were going to be two CSW staff already on the trip, I wanted to be sure my added presence would be worthwhile. "Merv, everywhere I go, you'll go!" he told me, so I agreed.

We flew into Erbil, which is the capital city of Iraqi Kurdistan and the largest city in northern Iraq. Erbil is very nice and appears like any modern European city. Around 200 miles north of Baghdad, it is known as one of the oldest continuously populated places on earth.

My flight had been delayed so we met for dinner at the hotel. There was me, Scot Bower our Chief Operations Officer and Wael Aleji from Syrian Christians for Peace; Frank and his policy advisor Abby Berg from 21st Century Wilberforce; and also on this trip, Todd Chasteen, Chief Legal Officer of Samaritan's Purse.

Samaritan's Purse were handling all the logistics for the trip, as they have a significant presence in Iraq. One of the first people we were introduced to was Matt Nowery, the Country Director for Northern Iraq, who actually lives in Erbil with his wife and children. Frank and I had already agreed that we would defer to Matt's local knowledge in every aspect of this trip. Security for the trip was entirely in his hands, and if on a particular day Matt said we couldn't go somewhere, then we didn't go. At dinner that first evening we met with Lise Grande the head of the UN humanitarian aid effort in Iraq who had travelled up from Baghdad and was able to give us an excellent briefing on all that was happening in the region. She spoke very highly of the work of Samaritans Purse.

Because we had a fairly large party we needed two, and sometimes three, cars to travel around in. Most of the time, myself, Frank and Todd travelled together, so Todd and I got to know each other well by spending many hours together on the road.

The first item on our itinerary was to visit the Kurdish city of Duhok in the far north, near to the Turkish and Syrian borders. En route, we stopped to visit two IDP (Internal Displaced People) camps.

The first was being run by Samaritan's Purse and was mainly for Yazidis.

The Yazidis are a people group whose history can be traced back to Mesopotamia – the region situated in the Tigris-Euphrates river system, that roughly corresponds to modern day Iraq and Kuwait. In terms of faith, they believe in one God who created the world, though their monotheistic beliefs are a mishmash of Christianity, Judaism, Islam and Zoroastrianism.

At the beginning of 2014, the Yazidis were targeted by the Islamic State of Iraq and the Levant (ISIL). ISIL attempted to eradicate the Yazidis in its efforts to rid the region of all non-Islamic influence. This act of terror was recognised by the US Congress, British Parliament and the EU as a genocide.

The situation began to erupt when hundreds of Yazidi families were threatened and given the choice of forced conversion to Sunni Islam or death. On August 3, 2014, ISIL militants attacked and took control of Sinjar, the main Yazidi town. Over the days that followed, thousands of Yazidis were murdered, and this led to around 200,000 people fleeing the area and being displaced from their homes. According to Iraqi government sources, on August 10, 2014, ISIL militants buried alive an unknown number of women and children in an onslaught that killed 500 people. Such atrocities were characteristic of these vile attacks.

The second camp we visited was mainly for Christians, this one being run by the Assyrian Aid Organisation. We couldn't stop long at either of these places, but at the second camp I was able to meet with a couple of Christian families and hear the stories of why they had been forced to flee their homes. Most of these had been living in or around Mosul. As it happened, according to news media Mosul had been "liberated" just the week before we arrived, but I soon learned that just because the Islamic State flag isn't flying over a city any more, it doesn't mean there aren't still IS people there. Liberated didn't mean safe. There were still regular fire fights and people were afraid to go outside.

I asked everyone I spoke to, "When Mosul is truly liberated and your house rebuilt, would you go back?"

Not a single person said yes. I spoke to one man who was a school teacher. He was now living in a small tent with his wife and their eight children. He told me that he might consider going back, but his wife was horrified by this and began screaming, "We are never going back!" She wouldn't even allow her 13-year old daughter go to the temporary school that had been set up in the camp, for fear of something happening to her. Sadly, young girls were routinely snatched, raped and trafficked.

We continued our journey northwest to Duhok and the next day we travelled southwest down to Sinjar city. We took the road close to the border, which meant we drove along the Turkish and Syrian borders (the Syrian border is just feet away), to arrive in Sinjar.

Our driver was a former Iraqi special forces soldier who had converted from Islam to Christianity. He was a great guy to have around and fun to be with, but you still knew you wouldn't want to get on the wrong side of him.

Travelling Iraq's roads was a constant stop-start affair as we passed through one roadblock after another. They came up every 10-20 miles or so. Thankfully, having an Iraqi driver together with Matt from Samaritans Purse meant that we were never detained for long and allowed to pass through. I noticed that many of the roadblocks were run by different factions. One would be flying the Iraqi military flag; the next would be controlled by the Peshmerga (literally "those who face death") – the Kurdistani forces; another would be run by PKK separatists; then there would be the NPU (Nineveh Plains Protection Units) – another military organisation run predominantly by Assyrian Christians. All of these groups have been fighting ISIL, but it's a very volatile situation, and once ISIL are gone, it's hard to guess what might happen.

In order to enter Sinjar city we crossed the Sinjar mountains – a 60-mile long mountain range that winds its way down, ending with a steep road that drops down into the city. Those final miles rank as one of the hairiest car rides I've ever had. It was one hairpin bend after another, with completely sheer drops.

As we topped the mountain, down in a valley a sea of tents could be seen, occupied by tens of thousands of Yazidis who had fled the city and taken refuge in the mountains. The Peshmerga had previously been in control of Sinjar city, but when they heard that ISIL was on their way to attack, they withdrew virtually overnight, leaving the citizens vulnerable. There was no defence of the city, no fighting; people grabbed what they could and ran up into the mountains pursued by ISIL. As we wound down the dangerous road into Sinjar, you could still see items of clothing strewn about the mountainside, where people had dropped their possessions as they ran.

The Yazidis are a very peaceful, loving people and they get along with Christian neighbours without any problem, so although Sinjar is a Yazidi town, there are two churches there. However, the whole city had been virtually demolished. The scale of the destruction was shocking. Everywhere had been bombed and burned. No building was left untouched. Now that ISIL had left, there were signs of a handful of people coming back and trying to live there again. I saw the incongruous sight of a man, who had tried to repair his bakery as best he could, baking bread as if everything had returned to normal. I couldn't help thinking, "Who on earth is he going to sell that bread to? There's no one here!"

We looked around Sinjar and explored an underground tunnel. This was a tunnel built by ISIL personnel and used as an escape route if anyone came looking for them. We needed to be extra careful whenever walking around as ISIL had booby trapped many areas with Improvised Explosive Devices (IED's).

On our way out of the region we stopped briefly in Lalish, the site of the Yazidi holy places, and met with their spiritual leader, Baba Sheikh. Heartbreakingly, he told us how his people had been robbed of all hope by the events of the past three years. He told us that up to 6,000 Yazidi women had been taken by ISIL and trafficked. Many had been rescued, but almost 3,000 were still missing.

* * *

The next few days were a real mixture of highs and lows as we travelled to some fascinating places, but also met people with harrowing personal stories.

One day we visited the city of Nimrud, 20 miles south of Mosul. Archaeologists believe that the city was named after Nimrod, the mighty hunter described in Genesis and Chronicles, who was the son of Cush, and therefore the great grandson of Noah. Sadly, in March 2015, ISIL had bombed and bulldozed their way through this ancient site, leaving very little evidence of the original city.

Back in Erbil I met a Christian young man called Sargon, who was just 14 years old. He is now living with his disabled mother. He was 11 when ISIL overran Mosul in August 2014. He tried to hide with his mother in their house, but eventually they ran out of food and ISIL fighters found them. They were told to either convert or die. His mother told him they should pretend to convert in order to survive. They did this, and although ISIL allowed them to live, Sargon was forcibly recruited as a fighter. He received military training and was forced to watch many executions of his fellow Christians. They are now unable to return to their hometown as no one trusts them. Could he seek refuge in the US or United Kingdom after fighting for ISIL? No one's situation is simple.

As Christians we must be very careful not to judge. In truth, none of us know what we would do, faced with such an horrific choice.

Then I met a Christian woman with a horrendous story. Let's call her Maryam. When ISIL attacked the Hamdanya area of Mosul three years earlier she was taken captive. After that she was trafficked 22 times – sold to 22 different men over a three-year period. She told me her story through an interpreter and she could recount the names of every man who had "owned" her, and the dates of her captivity. She had been raped hundreds of times and tried to escape on numerous occasions.

Once she jumped from a third floor window to get away from one man, but broke her leg. He simply came outside, dragged her back in, and gave her a severe beating. At one point she was tied to a post in the middle of the street with a "for sale" sign attached. Men would come by and lift up her clothes, so they could see what they might be buying.

As harrowing as all of that is, the worse part of the story is that she eventually escaped, using an underground railroad system set up by some US philanthropists, and made her way back to her family, but they rejected her because they said she had brought terrible shame upon them. Now she was living in a refuge apartment in Erbil, but was afraid to go outside, even in that relatively safe city.

She told her entire story impassively, sitting on a chair, not moving an inch, speaking in a steady voice, but what was particularly upsetting was that when she stopped, she completely broke down and wept. She then began screaming, "Please, get me out of here!" I don't think I've ever felt so helpless. As an organisation, we are working on trying to get her out of the country, but she is just one of thousands with similar stories.

* * *

On the last day we visited the Christian town of Qaraqosh, on the outskirts of Mosul. So many people's homes have been destroyed by the violence that it's hard to know where to begin to restore their lives. I saw churches that had been completely burnt out, with the crosses full of bullet holes. I saw a nunnery where the nuns had fled, leaving all their clothes still hanging in their wardrobes. Spent ammunition shells littered the courtyard because ISIL had used their compound for target practice.

At one point, we were looking at the remains of a burnt-out church when someone shouted, "Back to the cars! Now! Now!"

We all scrambled into our heavily armoured vehicles and left in such a rush that we ended up travelling the wrong way down a dual carriageway! It was a heart-racing few minutes until we got back on track and everything calmed down. We were never actually told what the danger had been.

Finally, they took us to the Samaritans Purse Field Hospital in Mosul. The place was very heavily guarded with extremely tight security and we were able to hear about the incredible work done by the amazingly dedicated medical team, mainly American young people who had put their lives on hold, in order to give extraordinary care to all who were brought to them – including ISIL soldiers.

Over 100 had died in their care, but they prided themselves that no one had ever actually died alone. The most harrowing sight for me was to see a 5-year old boy who had been brought in a few hours earlier. His right leg and lower stomach had been blown away when he trod on an IED whilst playing in the street. We all just broke down and wept.

The only place where we really found a vestige of hope was a small Evangelical church in Erbil – it truly was an oasis in the desert. The church had been planted by the Evangelical Alliance of Syria and Lebanon, and we were honoured to be accompanied by Pastor Sami Dagher, the visionary pioneer of the church. It was the one place we visited in the entire trip that didn't have its own security. People could just walk in off the street and it was filled with singing; choruses of joy and hope. We visited this church on the same day we'd met Maryam, so we told them about her situation and they insisted she come to them to be looked after. "We would never reject her," one of the leaders told us.

* * *

Going forward CSW will continue to monitor events in Iraq and the surrounding region closely, responding to any developments that have a bearing on FoRB. We have plans to work with Christian and Yazidi organisations, as well as to reach out to Arab and Kurdish communities, with the objective to empower religious minority communities to respond more effectively to violations of religious freedom. Training content for citizens will cover the history of religious freedom, documentation, advocacy, use of technology in advocacy, media advocacy and making use of local, national, and international human rights mechanisms.

20. USA

In 1997, while Baroness Caroline Cox was still working with CSW, she was awarded the William Wilberforce award, which was given annually by Chuck Colson of Prison Fellowship, on the eve of the US National Prayer Breakfast.

The Prayer Breakfast is a huge event that takes place in Washington D.C. each February and has been running since 1953. Around 3,500 people attend from 100 different nations. It was originally called the Presidential Prayer Breakfast, because the US President was always present, but the name was changed in the 1970s, although the President still does attend. The organisation of the event is a closely guarded secret, carried out by a group called The Fellowship Foundation – which in itself is an organisation shrouded in a degree of mystery. Each year the main speaker at the breakfast is kept secret, but previous speakers have included Bono, Mother Teresa and Tony Blair, to name a few.

The event is so popular that it's really difficult to get a ticket to attend unless someone personally invites you. Congressman Frank Wolf has invited me numerous times and, more recently, Senator John Barrasso of Wyoming. Even if you didn't have a ticket for the event, you could probably meet everyone you wanted to just by sitting in the lobby of the Hilton Hotel, where it has been held since the 1980s.

In 1997 I had a dilemma. Caroline Cox had an official invite to the Wilberforce award ceremony on the eve of the breakfast, and I was invited as her guest. The problem was I didn't have a ticket for the actual Prayer Breakfast itself, which began the next day. I wanted to attend, so I prayed about it and hoped that God would open some kind of door for me. He did just that, and in a quite miraculous way I never could have anticipated.

There was a large registration area for the breakfast, and it had a section for tickets that had been handed back because the person couldn't attend for some reason. I went there, but was told they had no spare tickets and I should come back and try again at 10:00pm that evening. I did, but was told, "Sorry, we haven't had any returned tickets this time." This was 10:00pm the night before the breakfast, so it didn't look as though I'd be able to attend.

I went back to my hotel room and, when I opened the door, I found an envelope on the floor with my name on it. Puzzled, I opened it up and found a ticket inside, along with a note. The note was from Charles Mendies, who I discovered was the Asian Co-ordinator for the prayer breakfast. I didn't know that he had that role, but I certainly knew the name Charles Mendies.

In the very early days of CSW, a trip was arranged to Nepal because we had heard that a large number of Christians had been imprisoned for their faith. David Atkinson MP was on the trip and at one point he was able to meet with the Chief of Police in Kathmandu, and indeed secure the release of the Christians. During their meeting the police chief said to David,

"You know, I am surprised to see you here."

"Why?" David asked.

"Well, I would never dream of putting a Jew in prison, because Jews around the world are so well organised. If one of their number was put in prison they would make my life very difficult until that person was released. I would never put a Muslim in prison for the same reason. But I can do whatever I like with Christians and no one says a word."

This was a shocking statement and one that made a huge impact on me. It made me more determined than ever never to lose an opportunity to speak up on behalf of Christians, wherever in the world they were being persecuted.

One of the Christians who had been imprisoned in Nepal at that time was Charles Mendies. His note to me said simply,

“Mervyn, you helped get me out of prison in Nepal once. I heard you were coming to the event, so here is a ticket for the prayer breakfast.”

That just blew me away.

Important connections

I remember that first prayer breakfast well for a number of reasons. At the Wilberforce Award dinner on the eve of the breakfast I was seated in between the President of a very large, well-known US Bible seminary, and a rather unassuming, quiet man. I asked the quiet man what he did and he answered in a matter of fact manner,

“Oh, I’m a philanthropist!”

He turned out to be Howard Ahmanson Jr. His father, Howard Sr., had founded an insurance and savings loan association and he made his fortune selling fire insurance and investing in real estate and oil. From the mid-1950s onwards Howard played an important role in the cultural life of Los Angeles, giving millions to many worthwhile projects.

Howard Jr. inherited his father’s home savings bank fortune and also became a philanthropist, funding numerous Christian and humanitarian causes.

Until I met Howard, I’d never heard of him. Many people haven’t, yet a few years ago Time Life magazine listed him and his wife, Roberta, at number 2 in the list of the top 50 most influential Christians in America. (Rick Warren was number 1 in case you’re wondering).

During the evening a guy came into the ballroom with a big entourage, being followed by at least half a dozen TV cameras. “Who’s this?” I wondered. "He seems pretty important!"

By virtue of having a seat on the top table, I got to speak to him briefly as he came to meet and greet all the dignitaries.

"Hi, nice to meet you," he said.

"Nice to meet you too," I replied, thinking, *I've still got no idea who this man is!*

After greeting numbers of people, he took to the podium and addressed the room, speaking for several minutes. Even while he was doing this, the penny still didn't drop. He finished his speech and sat down.

"Who was that?" I asked Howard.

"Well, that was Dr Billy Graham," he said dryly.

Somehow, despite having seen hundreds of images of Billy Graham, and indeed attended his meetings at Earls Court in 1966, I didn't recognise him that day. He seemed to look quite different.

CSW USA

During the trip, I got chatting with a group of three ladies and this proved to be a very significant meeting. They were all from Wyoming. One was Dr Anne Zimmerman, who was the daughter of Sir John Templeton, another great philanthropist who created the John Templeton Foundation. With Anne were Lisa Scaling and Betsy Vigneri.

They wanted to know all about the work of CSW and I spoke with them for quite a while. At the end I invited them to our London conference, which was due to take place in a couple of months. All three of them visited London in due course and told me that they felt called to help set up CSW in the USA – which is exactly what they did, locating the new US HQ in Casper, Wyoming. It was the beginning of a long and fruitful relationship. Sadly, Anne Zimmerman unexpectedly died in 2004, and although CSW still has an office in Casper, we now have a strong board in Washington DC, where much of our activity takes place. Lisa Scaling is the Chairman and Betsy Vigneri is the Secretary.

At this point in CSW's life, mainly due to Baroness Cox's involvement, we were undertaking relief work as well as advocacy. Caroline had a plan to introduce foster care to Russia, which at the time had a terrible system for managing orphans. At our London conference I mentioned that we would be setting up an orphanage and a foster care program, then we took an offering.

On the Monday after the conference one of our team was logging all the cash and cheques we'd received. As they finished, they found a scrap of paper, which they were about to discard thinking it was rubbish, but then noticed some writing. It was an IOU from Anne Zimmerman and her husband Gail, and simply said, "I owe you the cost of setting up foster care in Russia – Anne."

That little scrap of paper ended up being worth around half a million Pounds Sterling. Anne and her husband became faithful and generous supporters of CSW for years to come.

And as an added bonus, Casper, Wyoming, has become something of a second home to our family, and Lisa and Betsy, together with their husbands, Chip and Joe, have been wonderful hosts to us on many occasions. In fact, Chip and Joe hold the distinction of being the only people in the whole world who have ever persuaded me to go on a camping trip. We camped in the mountains above a town called Lander, and I experienced things that I never want to experience again in my life. And if you'd like to know more about our road trip back to Casper, and why we went via Muddy Gap, you'll need to ask Chip and Joe, as I'm sworn to secrecy!

So much came out of that very first prayer breakfast and I have attended nearly every year since. As it's held in February, I often get snowed in at Washington DC, waiting for my plane, but this is all part of the experience. It has been a big part of my life and has been amazing to see how God has used that event to put in place so many key connections that have facilitated the work of CSW over the years. Two people I providentially met at that first breakfast in 1997, Kit Webb and Cheryl Gardner, remain dear, firm friends, and have introduced me to innumerable key contacts over time.

During 1997 and 1998, when I travelled to Washington DC, I was privileged to witness Congressman Frank Wolf drafting the International Religious Freedom Act (IRFA). This act of Congress established the United States Commission on International Religious Freedom and the State Department Office of International Religious Freedom.

Since that time, I've seen how The USA has led the way in the area of international religious freedom. Even during 2018, the US Secretary of State invited the foreign ministers of 80 nations to attend a Ministerial, with the sole purpose of advancing international religious freedom.

All of this activity has come out of Frank Wolf's congressional bill. It underlines to me the importance of NGOs, like CSW, who take politicians and journalists on trips to countries where they can see the true state of religious freedom for themselves. Frank himself would say that the trip we undertook together to Romania in 1985 was a catalyst for his life's work, culminating in the IRFA bill, and all the good it has proliferated since. In fact, another of those we took to Romania in 1985, Congressman Chris Smith, has also spent his whole political life tirelessly fighting for international religious freedom, and whenever we meet we always reminisce about our time together in Romania – especially those sheep's brains, eh Chris?!

21. Provision

Stories of such miraculous provision leads me on to talk about the countless ways in which God has supernaturally provided for the ministry at just the right time. What happened with Seth's money box savings, mentioned earlier, is a microcosm of what the Lord has done time and again on a bigger scale.

In an earlier chapter I made mention of the period when Roger Shelley was CSW's National Director. In those early days I was Chairman of the Board, but I also kept the books. Even though he was responsible for leading the work, Roger left that side of things to me and I was always the one who knew how much was in the bank. (Incidentally, if you ask Sina our Finance Director, he'll tell you I still am!)

Our main office was the spare room in Roger's house in Olivia Drive, Leigh-on-Sea. I lived 20 miles away in Grays and very often I would drive to his house to hand deliver his salary cheque. Anyone who has run a ministry will know that you can be as practical as you like, but there is always an element of faith involved. If we had all the resources we needed to do everything we wanted to do, how would that glorify God? Ultimately, we must depend upon Him.

On one occasion, we got to the end of the month and there was not enough to pay Roger's salary, which at that time was around £1,400 plus several pence. I thought, "Oh no, what are we going to do?" but I immediately received a peace from God about it and had the strong impression that I should write out the cheque and give it to Roger, regardless.

I wrote out the cheque, got in the car and set off for Roger's. When I arrived, the first thing I did was to hand him the cheque, without a word. Roger said,

"Oh, I'm glad you've come today. Look what just arrived in the post."

We had recently sent out an issue of our magazine, *Response*. This issue featured a story about some Romanian pastors who were in prison and we made a financial appeal. The letter Roger had received was from a young couple who were moved by the story and had sent a gift. They were recently married and had been saving up for a new suite of furniture for their house, but when they read the story, just like Seth they said, "Christians in Romania need our money more than we need a new suite," so they emptied their savings account and mailed us a cheque. Amazingly, to the pound, it equalled the sum of the cheque I had just given to Roger.

This was the first time that it really hit me: *God was committed to providing for this ministry and He would meet our needs.*

God continued to step in when we really needed Him and provided in lots of ways – often with very large amounts of money arriving quite unexpectedly or being provided through key connections He had initiated.

On one occasion, a couple based in Greece who had been left a large inheritance were visiting friends in Birmingham. While they were there, they saw our *Response* magazine on the coffee table and began reading it. Soon after they sent us an incredibly generous gift of £100,000.

However, the young member of staff who was asked to bank the cheque had never seen a cheque that big before and mistakenly wrote out the bank deposit slip as £100. Fortunately, we managed to clear this up quickly with the bank! This was the largest donation we had ever received and was an amazing encouragement to us all.

It was around the March of 1999 that I gave up my job at *Sweet'n Low* in order to work for CSW full time. I had to give six months' notice and was nearing the end of the notice period when Stuart Windsor phoned me up and said,

"Merv, we haven't got enough money to pay the staff this month."

I was shocked. I remember coming off the phone to Stuart and saying to Wendy,

"What on earth is God doing? I've just given up my job and there's no money to pay anyone, let alone me!" I guess I expected Wendy to react quite badly to that, but instead she said,

"What do you mean, 'What is God doing?' He's just saying, 'Do you trust me?'"

Of course, she was quite right. It was February time, and shortly after this we had our annual conference in London. At the conference I found myself chatting to one of our supporters, who told me that he lived near me, and suggested it might be good to meet up and pray together. I told him I'd like to and that was the beginning of a lovely prayer partnership which went on for a number of years until he moved away from the area.

At the conference it had been announced that I was to be CSW's new Chief Executive, and the first time we got together to pray, my friend brought it up.

"It's great news that you're going to be Chief Executive," he said.

"Thank you," I said.

Then he added,

"I've been putting some money away for CSW in a little fund for a while now, but I've never felt the time was right to hand it over. But when I heard that you were to become Chief Executive, I felt that I needed to give it now."

"That's very kind of you," I told him. "How much are we talking about?"

"Oh, I think it's about a hundred," he said.

I thought to myself,

"Well, that's nice, but it's not a lot – £100!"

It turned out to be £100,000! It was God's way of saying to me,

"Now do you trust me?"

I can't tell you that I've never worried about money since, but I've always known that if push came to shove, God would provide when we really needed it.

* * *

Sometimes God will take what appears to be a disaster and turn it into something unexpectedly wonderful. While I was still Chairman of CSW and Stuart Windsor was National Director, we provided him with a company car. It was a not-very-salubrious Vauxhall Astra, but it was what our finances would stretch to. Stuart was famous for travelling the length and breadth of the country continuously, and he also commuted every week to the new CSW office in Witney from his home in Widnes, so it made sense to give him a vehicle.

If he needed to go into London, however, Stuart would often take the train, and one day I received a distressed phone call from him.

"Merv, I left my car at Oxford station this morning and it's been stolen!" he said.

"Right, OK," I said, "that's a bit of a disaster."

I knew Stuart couldn't function without a car, so I told him to hire one for the time being. But Stuart told me about a Christian who owned a car dealership, and who he'd met years before when he was pastoring in Widnes, though he couldn't remember the man's name.

"I'm sure he was from the Newmarket area," he told me. "I'm going to try and track him down."

The next day I was in the office at *Sweet'n Low* (which was just a few miles from Newmarket) and my phone rang. The receptionist said,

"Merv, I've got a Mr Heffer on the phone for you." I didn't recognise the name at all.

"Who is he?" I asked.

"He says he's the Dealer Principal from Heath Ford Motors in Newmarket."

"OK, put him through," I said. Paul Heffer came on the phone and said,

"Stuart Windsor has phoned me and given me your name. He said I need to speak to you because you're the Chairman of his organisation. Can you come and see me this afternoon?"

"Actually, I can't," I told him, "this afternoon I've got to go and look at a car with my wife. She's nursing in Cambridge and needs a car to get around."

"Forget about that," Paul breezed, "I'll find your wife a car. Just come over and see me."

I went to see Paul and got the full story from him. Stuart had phoned around the car dealerships in the Newmarket area, saying,

"Look, I don't know the guy's name, but does the chap who owns your garage talk about Jesus all the time?"

After puzzling a number of sales staff, one person said, "Oh yeah, that's Paul Heffer," and put Stuart through to him. On hearing about Stuart's dilemma, Paul had immediately given instructions for a Ford Sierra to be put on a pick-up truck and delivered to Witney. He told Stuart,

"You can use that for as long as you like, and I'll find you a new car in the meantime."

Paul and I got on really well and became very close friends and prayer partners (he and his wife Norma are godparents to Seth). He sourced Wendy a really good, cheap car, and whenever it went into the garage to be serviced there was rarely any bill, which was incredibly kind of him.

Paul is the sort of guy who will strike up a conversation with anyone and one day he spotted a man in a hotel lobby with a fish badge on his lapel. He could see the man had a sheet of headed notepaper in front of him, that Paul immediately recognised as one of his suppliers. Paul brazenly approached the guy and said,

"Hi, I'm Paul Heffer and you and I have two things in common: we both love Jesus, and we both have the same supplier." Surprised, the man said,

"Well, you're right, I do love Jesus, but I'm actually the Managing Director of your supplier."

He and Paul chatted for a long while. Paul said that he'd like to introduce him to me and, in due course, the three of us met and had a meal together. We got along famously and he too became a good friend. In due course he would become a great supporter of CSW and, unknowingly, help us out at a critical time.

At different times in the history of CSW, like any organisation, we've had cash flow crises and, again, God has bailed us out. At one time, our former finance director hadn't informed me about the serious state of our cash flow situation and I suddenly learned one month that we were around £30,000 short.

I didn't sleep well that night and woke up about 3.00am thinking about the situation. "How did we get to this position? And more to the point, what are we going to do?" I got up there and then and read my Bible. I happened to turn to the verse Philippians 4:19, which says,

"And this same God who takes care of me will supply all your needs from his glorious riches, which have been given to us in Christ Jesus." (NLT)

I decided I couldn't sleep, so leaving Wendy in dreamland I drove into work at 4.30am, typed that verse out and printed it in large letters and put it on the wall of my office (where it has been ever since). I knew that God was telling me He would provide, one way or another.

I took some immediate action to cut certain costs – cancelling purchases that we were going to make, etc. But I realised, not for the first time, that we wouldn't have enough cash to pay all our staff at the end of the month. Right then I had to decide two things. The first was, should I warn our staff that they might not get paid this month? The second was, Wendy and I were about to go on holiday with the kids. We had planned a trip to a caravan site in France and were due to leave within days. Should we go?

I prayed about the matter and immediately felt the peace of God wash over me. I had such peace that God would help us, that I didn't tell the staff and we did indeed go on holiday. Only me, and the senior leadership team knew about the situation.

The day before we had to pay everyone's salaries I received a message from the office, while I was still on holiday. It was a simple text saying that morning we had received a gift of £30,000, and on enquiry I found it had been sent by Paul's supplier friend. It was the first gift he'd given us (and I'd never asked him for money) and I have no idea why it was that amount – other than that was the exact amount we needed! My friend David Shearman often says, "God is never late, but He rarely takes the opportunity to be early." Once again, His timing was perfect, and my faith had been stretched and grown a little more.

That particular year was a very bad year for us financially – probably the worst we ever had – but again the Lord rescued us at the eleventh hour. A few years previously I had taken Paul Heffer to the National

Prayer Breakfast in London, and while we were there he introduced me to Peter Vardy (now Sir Peter), the owner of the national car dealerships carrying his name. To cut a long story short I had asked Peter if he could make us an interest free loan to help us with cash flow. He did so, but told me that the Trust he was taking it from needed it to be repaid in one year's time. When the one year was up I asked Peter to extend the deadline, which he did, but made it clear there could be no more extensions. The loan became due for repayment in December and, to be honest, we were close to insolvency. In fact, we needed to raise £100k before the year end. After much prayer I felt God was telling me to actually ask Peter to convert the £50k loan into a gift. In fear and trepidation, I emailed Peter with the ask. Within minutes the reply came back from Peter's phone saying, "OK, it's yours!" He had no idea that the gift actually saved us. Of course, a £50k loan converted to a gift made £100k difference on our balance sheet. Praise the Lord.

More key connections

It was at a CSW conference around 15 years ago that a Canadian man I'd never met before came to talk to me. When you are fronting a conference, all kinds of people come to chat to you about all manner of things – some more significant than others. This man asked me for my business card and said to me,

"I know you're really busy and everyone wants to talk to you, but I'd like to give you my card and get in touch with you after the conference."

I had a habit of putting people's business cards in my suit pocket and forgetting about them, but I thanked him for his card and put it in my wallet – as if to acknowledge that this one was significant.

His name was James Reimer. A couple of months later I received an email from him which I nearly accidentally deleted, simply because I'd forgotten who he was, and the subject of the email was simply "Gift" so it looked a bit odd! James was emailing to tell me that he was coming to London and asking if we could meet for lunch.

I arranged lunch at the Atrium, opposite Parliament, the haunt of many parliamentarians and journalists, which has now turned into a coffee shop. James and I really hit it off and ended up having a three-hour lunch. James' father, Dr D.S. Reimer, had established Reimer Express, which was one of the largest haulage companies in Canada. Dr Reimer had suffered from pre-stroke symptoms requiring James to take over the management of the company for quite a while. In addition to this he was a financial consultant and was in the UK advising a member of the Royal family.

Jim told me that when he was at the conference, listening to me speak, he thought, "I'd like to get to know this guy." His family gave away large amounts of money, and Jim really had a heart to help the persecuted church. He had been going to set up his own NGO to do something, but then discovered CSW existed and was already doing what he was interested in. He had identified three different organisations to support and CSW was one of them. At the end of our meeting he said to me,

"I came here to meet the CEO of CSW and I've gone away with a new friend."

Not only have we become very close friends, but our families too, with Jim's wife Sandy, and Wendy and Seth all being part of our strong relationship.

Jim is not only very generous in his faithful giving to CSW, but is a great strategist, and lots of the ideas I've had over the years have been a result of his wisdom. He's also an amazing encourager and I always come away from our regular lunches together feeling affirmed, inspired and energised.

Jim helped me to set up something we initially called the "Brown envelope fund". His heart is not just for advocacy, but also for humanitarian aid for those suffering persecution. CSW focuses on advocacy, not aid, but I told him that when our staff go overseas, they often take a brown envelope with a small amount of cash in it. That envelope is for any immediate need they see that they want to help with.

Jim said that he'd love to give us some money so that we could have a small "brown envelope" style fund. If anyone came to us for emergency practical aid, we could then respond with some immediate assistance. Jim and I control the fund together and when staff come to me with requests I email them to him to authorise. In practice Jim has never turned down one of my requests. "I trust you to do what's right," he tells me.

Over the past couple of years CSW has changed its senior leadership structure and I have passed the operational control over to my friend and very dependable, competent colleague, Scot Bower, in order for me to concentrate on all external relations. During this changeover period, James played a key role in offering me advice and support. I also believe Jim's influence on me, and on the world of religious freedom generally, will increase over the years to come.

22. Religious Liberty

In 2005 I received an invitation to go to a meeting in Amsterdam arising out of the Lausanne Movement. It was interesting to me because the invitation came from Johan Companjen, who had worked very closely with Brother Andrew and went from being his bag carrier to the International President of Open Doors. There was to be a two-day consultation and it was strictly for the CEOs of the invited organisations – they wouldn't accept deputies in the place of the main leader. I was intrigued by this and accepted the invitation.

For those unfamiliar with the Lausanne Movement, its history goes back over 40 years. It grew out of the 1974 International Congress on World Evangelisation, which was held in Lausanne, Switzerland, and organised in part by Billy Graham. More than 2,500 representatives from 150 nations gathered to discuss and promote evangelism.

During its 2004 gathering, held in Thailand, a Persecuted Church Forum concluded that those organisations working to promote religious liberty would be able to do so more effectively if there was a formal way of collaborating. The forum recommended that a network be established in order to facilitate those organisations to work together. This was the beginning of what would be called the Religious Liberty Partnership.

When I arrived in Amsterdam, the CEOs of about a dozen organisations were in attendance. Brian O'Connell, an American from Seattle, had been brought in to steer the meeting. Although we'd never met before, I recognised Brian's name from his involvement with the Evangelical Alliance's Religious Liberty Commission, and I soon realised this was a man who shared the same passion for partnership and for religious freedom as me.

The meeting began, and a long discussion ensued with lots of different people expressing their points of view on the complex matters which we were all dealing with in our own separate ways. I stayed quiet for a long time and didn't speak at all for the first few hours, but eventually I felt that I had something to say.

I gave an impassioned speech about the fact that all our organisations survived on donations, and we all felt there was a limited pot of money that we were competing for. This made it difficult for us to truly collaborate, because each organisation was overly concerned about funding for their own infrastructure. But, if we truly wanted to achieve something for the wider cause of religious freedom, then we needed to *really* work together.

"It's not a finite pot of money," I said, "it's an *infinite* pot, because it's all God's money. And I believe that if we all work together, we are likely to get more money, because it's God's desire for us that we do so."

I was surprised that a number of people broke into spontaneous applause and thought that I must have hit the right note.

Progress was made and at the end of those two days it was agreed to formally set up the Religious Liberty Partnership; also that we should appoint Brian O'Connell as our Facilitator and, at the very least, have an annual CEO-level consultation. Each member organisation would pay an annual membership fee and there would be a five-person leadership team. We were each asked to write down five names of people we thought could lead the group. Again, to my total surprise, I was voted onto the leadership team. The five of us met together before we went home, and I was humbled again when the others asked me to be chairman of the group.

It was a great honour to take on this role, but I really believed in what the RLP was setting out to do, and it's been a great joy to lead the group since that time. The wider group meet once a year and we vary the venue between western nations and developing countries. Some of the countries that have hosted consultations have included Switzerland, USA, Canada and the UK, but also Thailand, Brazil, Cyprus, Sri Lanka, Turkey and, in 2019, we will be convening in Nigeria.

The most important work that takes place at each consultation is not done in the excellent plenary sessions, but during the lunch and coffee breaks, when people interact with each other. Every single year new partnerships between member organisations are formed, and the fight against religious persecution is the better for it. Over the years, a number of Task Forces have also been formed covering such subjects as the Apostasy Laws, Early Warnings of Persecution, and Gendered Religious Persecution.

One of the really key tasks the RLP has undertaken has been to put together a Code of Best Practices in working together, which is reviewed and, if necessary, updated each year. This is comprehensive and really useful for any Christian organisation, not just for RLP members. Some principles covered in the document include Doing no Harm, Communication, Accountability, and Ethical Fundraising and Data Collection. A copy can be found at https://rlpartnership.org/wp-content/uploads/2018/05/RLP-Best-Practices-April-2018.pdf

Of course, over the years wonderful personal relationships have been formed, and an added benefit is that when, as happens from time to time, issues arise between organisations, the CEO's can pick up the phone to each other and work things through together.

We now have something like 70 members from 25 nations. As an organisation we exist to facilitate collaboration, so while we don't do a lot of hands-on work, many bilateral and multilateral partnerships are formed in order to work on specific projects.

Over the past few years, starting at our consultation in Oxford, the RLP has made some strategic changes, moving its emphasis from just persecuted Christians to the wider concept of Freedom of Religion or Belief (FORB) for people of all faiths and none. Of course, that is a position CSW has held for some years.

A change in our statement of faith (from the Lausanne Covenant to the Apostle's Creed) is similarly a reflection of our desire to be a space where all Christian organisations can come together and explore the benefits of collaboration.

One year, our annual consultation was held in Sri Lanka. We had links there already, with Godfrey Yogarajah, who headed the Evangelical Alliance of Sri Lanka, and who also runs the World Evangelical Alliance Religious Liberty Commission, and indeed is now the Deputy Secretary General of WEA. The event was held in the Galle Face hotel in Colombo, which is a wonderful old colonial building right on the beach.

One of the people I met at the conference was a remarkable lady called Lalani Jayasinghe, who had come to share her testimony with the gathering. This was in 2010, and her story goes back to 1989.

The man who would become Lalani's husband was Lionel Jayasinghe, a Buddhist monk who lived in a part of southern Sri Lanka where there wasn't a single church in a fifty-mile radius. One day he was walking down a dusty back road when a car drove past him and out of the car window a piece of paper fluttered into the air and landed at his feet. He bent down and picked it up and discovered it was a Gospel tract. He was immediately impacted by the words he read and gave his heart to Christ there and then.

This set Lionel on a journey to follow Jesus and attend the Assemblies of God Bible College based in Colombo. While there, he met Lalani, another student, and in due course they married. After graduation, Lionel passionately wanted to return to the area where he'd previously been a monk and plant a church in that spiritually dry region. Together they began a church and subsequently their son was born.

The church grew slowly because this was a very hard area. When their son was two years old, there were still only a handful of members in the church, but it was beginning to grow.

One day, as Lionel was working in the yard of their house, a man appeared, pulled a gun from inside his clothing and shot Lionel. Lionel staggered into the house bleeding, but the man pursued him and stabbed him to death in front of Lalani and their toddler.

Following this devastating tragedy, friends and staff at the AoG college pleaded with Lalani to return to Colombo, where they could look after her and her son, but she refused.

"No, both Lionel and I were called to this area. I'm staying."

The first cross ever to be seen in that part of Sri Lanka was the one placed on Lionel's grave. For the next 20 years Lalani continued to pastor that church. On more than one occasion she was stoned. The church was bombed and had to be rebuilt. Several times it was set on fire and had to be repaired or partially rebuilt.

One incident after another occurred, but each time Lalani refused to call the police. Instead, she deliberately sought out the perpetrators of the crime and told them that she forgave them. Even the man who had killed her husband.

Today, her original little church, where Lionel was killed, has around 500 members and she has planted a number of other churches in the area. Now when you drive into her town, the very first thing you see is the huge neon cross on the side of her church building. I invited Lalani to come and speak at CSW's annual conference the following year.

This is just one example of the hundreds of thousands of extraordinary people around the world who are choosing to live out their faith under extreme pressures that most of us will never truly understand or have to face in our lifetime. It's another reason why we are choosing to fight for the freedom to express faith – for people like Lalani.

23. Everyone. Free to Believe

When CSW began back in 1979, our focus was very much on Eastern Europe, particularly Romania and Russia. At the time those countries were very hard places for Christians to live. At the end of 1989, when the Berlin Wall was brought down – perhaps the most visible, physical representation of the Iron Curtain – it symbolised the fall of communism across Europe. We wondered briefly if there was a long-term future for CSW in the wake of these events, but of course, we soon discovered that there were countless other believers being persecuted in other parts of the world.

Work we carried out in Burma (Myanmar), and subsequently in Pakistan and Sudan had alerted us to the fact that it wasn't only Christians who were suffering. People of other faiths were being persecuted and killed for their faith too.

Initially, CSW worked on behalf of Christians in Burma, such as the Karen, Karenni, Chin and Kachin peoples, who were suffering very badly at the hands of the Burmese military regime. But suffering alongside these Christians were a group called the Rohingya Muslims (this was way back in 1999, when no one had even heard of the Rohingya). As followers of Christ, it was clear we could not simply ignore what was happening to this Muslim group. We had to stand up and speak out for them too.

We were faced with a similar situation in India, where Muslims were being persecuted alongside Christians by fundamentalist Hindus; in Pakistan where both Hindu's, Christians and Ahmadiyya Muslims were persecuted; in Iran where adherents of the Bahá'í faith continued to suffer; and in Sudan where Muslims who did not adhere to the version of Islam espoused by the ruling party were attacked alongside Christian communities in the Nuba Mountains.

Article 18 of the UN Declaration of Human Rights says,

Everyone has the right to freedom of thought, conscience and religion; this right includes freedom to change his religion or belief, and freedom, either alone or in community with others and in public or private, to manifest his religion or belief in teaching, practice, worship and observance.

Simply put, that gives everyone the right to choose, to change, and to practise their religion privately and publicly. That right is also articulated in the International Covenant on Civil and Political Rights (ICCPR) which, unlike the UNHDR, is binding on countries which are signed up to it.

So that's what is in the international statutes, but what does the Bible say about it?

The biblical narrative

CSW's advocates understood the theological reason for advocating for FORB and had been teaching it for years, but not everyone in the organisation fully comprehended it – me included, if I'm honest!

At the end of 2016, I received a phone call from my old friend, Joel Edwards, former General Director of the Evangelical Alliance and CEO of Micah Challenge Global. Joel was about to embark on his doctorate studies at Durham University and was considering his thesis. He told me he would like to investigate Christian involvement in human rights and asked if he could come into CSW's office one day each week to interview me and the staff.

Joel began this project in January 2017 and, after a few weeks, came to talk to me.

"I really love this organisation," he said. "Could I volunteer on a regular basis?"

Together we made a plan that Joel would continue his one day per week research, but volunteer for another day each week. I thought this was a great opportunity for me personally, and us as an organisation to get to grips with the theology of FORB, so I asked him to spend time with all the staff, examining the theological basis for championing the religious freedom of those of all faiths and none.

Joel did a great job on this, leading several debate sessions where people could air their views and ask questions. After a few weeks we all (not just the advocates) fully embraced the theology of FORB.

There are numerous verses in the Bible that give insight into God's heart for all people. Leviticus 19:33-34 says, *"Do not take advantage of foreigners* [someone of another religion] *who live among you in your land. Treat them like native-born Israelites, and love them as you love yourself."*

God makes the point that His people were foreigners in another land at one point in their history, so they should not mistreat the foreigners living among them. Exodus 22:21 says, *"You must not exploit or oppress a foreign resident..."* and Deuteronomy 10:19 instructs God's people to *"love those who are foreigners."*

Some of the most challenging verses in the Bible are Proverbs 31:8-9 (NLT), which urge us to,

"Speak up for those who cannot speak for themselves; ensure justice for those being crushed. Yes, speak up for the poor and helpless, and see that they get justice."

This principle has to be at the heart of all we do. The scripture doesn't limit this to Christians; it's a carte blanche command.

In Luke's gospel, Jesus has an exchange with an expert in the law (Luke 10:25-37), in which he tells the parable of the Samaritan – an illustration sparked by the question "Who is my neighbour?" This striking, counter-cultural illustration turns the world on its head for the legal expert.

A traditional interpretation of the word used for neighbour is *rey'a* in Hebrew and *pleysios* in Greek, meaning "near or close one". However, Jesus makes it clear that "neighbour" includes everyone, even the Samaritan, who the Jewish audience would have identified as a foreigner at best and an enemy at worst.

The expert in the law is undone by the story of the caring "Good" Samaritan, and Jesus tells him to "go and do likewise". In other words, go and care for the foreigner, the one who is not like you, the one you distrust and avoid. They are now your neighbour.

Some time ago, the Bible Society carried out an experiment in Reading town centre and filmed it covertly. Quite simply, they wanted to see who might be prepared to lend their mobile phone to a vicar, as opposed to a rough sleeper. Most people's reactions were predictable, yet a few stood out as being amazing, kind people.

The idea of loving everyone and doing good to them is a concept some find difficult and Christians have sometimes erroneously used Galatians 6:10 – *"Therefore, whenever we have the opportunity, we should do good to everyone – especially to those in the family of faith"* – as a reason to only assist fellow Christians.

However, the first half of this verse clearly instructs us to do good to *everyone.* Everyone, regardless of their faith.

Practically speaking, can you imagine taking a truckload of grain into a famine-stricken area and only giving it to Christians, when people of other faiths are starving alongside them? It would be utterly inhumane to give bread to Christian children and send other children away hungry. We are all made in the image of God.

Free will

God has given us free will, as is made clear throughout Scripture, and this is a critical factor in deciding to support those who follow other faiths. We may not agree with their choices, but we must defend their right to choose. In his *Desiring God* blog John Piper wrote the following:

"Our will is free if our preferences and our choices are really our own in such a way that we can justly be held responsible for whether they are good or bad. The opposite would be that our preferences and choices are not our own, but that we are robots or puppets with no meaningful acts of preferring or choosing."

God has given us the free will to choose Him or reject Him. Of course, He wants us to choose Him, but He doesn't force us to do so. However, one of the great challenges to religious freedom comes from individuals or institutions that seek to enforce a uniform belief and to punish anyone who changes their religion or belief. Although the Quran does not prescribe death for apostasy, Islamic theologians who supported the death penalty have justified it using the Hadith. In some countries, anyone is allowed to kill an apostate, even a family member.

I once had an interesting conversation with an Afghani who was a Professor at Kabul University. We met at a religious freedom conference in London, and I asked him,

"Do you believe in the whole of Article 18?"

"Yes, of course," he replied.

"So, you believe in people's right to change religion?"

"Yes," he replied, "I believe that everyone should be able to convert to Islam."

The "right to change" was a good thing, in his opinion, as long as it meant conversion *to* Islam and not *from* Islam

"What about the other way around?" I asked him.

"No, no, I could never agree to that," he said. "The Quran forbids it." But then he said to me,

"It's just the same as the way the Bible forbids Christians to convert to another religion."

"Well, you better show me that verse in the Bible," I told him, "because I've never seen it. It doesn't exist, because God has given everyone free will. He doesn't force us to believe."

He was completely staggered by this and asked me,

"So what would you say then if a Christian friend of yours became a Muslim?"

"Well, first of all I would pray for them, and I would be disappointed, but I would defend to the hilt their right to choose."

In a gentle way we are endeavouring to help our supporters understand why we believe it's right to speak up for those of other faiths who are suffering injustice. I'm not a syncretistic Christian who believes there are many different routes to God, but I do believe we are all made in God's image, which means every human being has an inherent dignity, and each one has been given a free will. When I speak about this topic in churches, the vast majority embrace it and are enthusiastic that we are actively showing the love of Christ to those of other faiths. Despite this, I occasionally hear people say, "But you're endorsing another religion!" I am not, I'm endorsing the right of other human beings to choose their religion or belief, or to have no belief at all, because God has given that choice to them.

What we do can be both puzzling and eye opening for those we seek to help and defend. We set out to help a man in Indonesia called Alexander Aahn, who was imprisoned for expressing his atheist convictions online. Our East Asia advocate, Ben Rogers, visited him in prison. When Ben arrived and told him who he was, Alexander said,

"You must have made a mistake."

"What do you mean?" Ben asked.

"Didn't anyone tell you why I'm in prison? It's because I'm an atheist."

"I know that," Ben said.

"But you're a Christian."

"Yes."

"So why have you come to see me?"

"Because I'm a Christian."

It took a while for Alexander to grasp that the love of Christ was the motivating factor, and that his personal beliefs, or lack of religion or belief, wouldn't deter a Christian from advocating for his right to choose. Ben has visited Alexander a number of times now and they have a wonderful friendship.

This is a microcosm of the bigger picture – and the bigger picture is that we are advocating for religious freedom for all faiths, *because we are Christians.*

One of the most persecuted religious groups in the world is the Ahmadiyya Muslim community. Annually, they hold a "Jalsa Salana" festival, where some 30,000 adherents from all around the world gather for a few days in fields just a stone's throw from my home in Farnham. I have been privileged on more than one occasion to address this group, whose wonderful motto is "Love for all, hatred for none". I have been able to assure them that, as Christians, we at CSW would always stand with them in their persecution. By doing this I believe I am obeying the words in 1 John 3:18, where we are told not just to love with our words, but in action and truth.

I once heard Brother Andrew say that, for Christians the word Islam should stand for "I Sincerely Love All Muslims", which really made an impact on me. I don't love the Muslim faith, but I do love all Muslims, as I love all atheists, Hindus, Yazidis, Buddhists and others – regardless of their religion or belief. That is what the Christian faith is about, loving your neighbour as yourself, and doing good to all.

In Matthew 5:44 Jesus tells us to love our enemies and pray for those who persecute us. The apostle Paul elaborated on this command when he wrote,

"Bless those who persecute you; bless and do not curse..." (Romans 12:14)

This calls for radical, counter-intuitive behaviour. When someone is persecuting us on account of our faith, instead of retaliating, we should intentionally be good to them.

I can think of no better example of this than my friend Reverend Yunusa Nmadu, CEO of CSW Nigeria, and current General Secretary of ECWA (one of the largest denominations in northern Nigeria.) Yunusa used to pastor a church in Kaduna, the capital of Kaduna State in north-western Nigeria. The church is in a predominantly Muslim neighbourhood. It was regularly destroyed during religious tension and the congregation would build it up again and continue to use it.

There was little interaction with the community. Yunusa decided this needed to change. He persuaded his church to purchase food stuffs that would be donated to the poorest families in six surrounding mosques, so they could break their Ramadan fasts. He then approached the local traditional ruler, who received him enthusiastically and organised a meeting that was attended by local press, and representatives from the church and the mosques, where the food was handed over.

The next time there were religious tensions in the area, Muslim youth protected the church premises.

Not only that, but while Yunusa was pastoring the church, this event turned into a yearly gathering known as "Friendship Day". Local

Muslim dignitaries and community members would visit the church for Sunday services, then everyone would eat together before food stuffs were donated to the neediest families.

This reconciliation was possible only because the church decided to bless those who were persecuting them through a positive act of faith.

This is radical Christian living. As I see that same radical Christ-like love expressed daily in the work of the amazing, committed and passionate team at CSW, I look forward to seeing how our love in action will change the world!

Get Involved

CSW is a Christian human rights organisation specialising in freedom of religion or belief around the world, and as Christians we stand with everyone facing injustice because of their religion or belief.

CSW's team of specialist advocates work on over 25 countries across Africa, Asia, Latin America and the Middle East, to ensure that the right to freedom of religion or belief is upheld and protected. Our vision is a world free from religious persecution, where everyone can practise a religion or belief of their choice.

The right to freedom of religion or belief is also known as the "first freedom" given to humanity by God. It's a touchstone human right, often serving as a "litmus test" for whether other rights are at risk of being abused.

It's a right we must protect, defend and restore.

CSW seeks to challenge and change the laws, behaviours and policies which lead to abuses of the right to freedom of religion and belief. We have four decades of experience advocating for freedom of religion or belief around the world.

Whether it's campaigning for us, involving your church, volunteering, fundraising or taking part in one of our many events each year, your support really helps.

Your voice holds unimaginable power and can save lives.

To find out how you can make a difference, visit:

https://www.csw.org.uk/getinvolved.htm